¡Gracias!

A LATIN AMERICAN JOURNAL

OTHER BOOKS BY HENRI J. M. NOUWEN

Intimacy

Creative Ministry

With Open Hands

The Wounded Healer

Thomas Merton: Contemplative Critic

Aging: The Fulfillment of Life
(with Walter J. Gaffney)

Out of Solitude

Reaching Out

The Genesee Diary

The Living Reminder

Clowning in Rome

In Memoriam

The Way of the Heart

Making All Things New

A Cry for Mercy

Compassion
*(with Donald P. McNeill
and Douglas A. Morrison)*

A Letter of Consolation

¡Gracias!

A LATIN AMERICAN JOURNAL

Henri J. M. Nouwen

HARPER & ROW, PUBLISHERS, SAN FRANCISCO

1817

Cambridge, Hagerstown, New York, Philadelphia
London, Mexico City, São Paulo, Sydney

Excerpts from "A Cry for Latin America" are reprinted by permission of the *National Catholic Reporter*, P.O. Box 281, Kansas City, MO 64141.

All Bible quotations are from the Jerusalem Bible except the following. The quotations from Isaiah and Hebrews are taken from the New American Bible, copyright © 1970 by the Confraternity of Christian Doctrine, Washington, D.C., and used by permission of copyright owner. All rights reserved. Quotations from the Psalms are from *The Psalms: A New Translation,* © The Grail 1963. Used by permission of The Grail, England.

FIRST EDITION

Designed by Catherine Hopkins

Library of Congress Cataloging in Publication Data

Nouwen, Henri J. M.
GRACIAS! : A LATIN AMERICAN JOURNAL.

    1. Nouwen, Henri J. M. 2. Spiritual life—Catholic authors. 3. Catholic Church—Clergy—Biography. 4. Bolivia—Description and travel—1981– . 5. Peru—Description and travel—1981– . 6. Vocation, Ecclesiastical. I. Title.
BX4705.N87A34 1983   282'.092'4 [B]   82–48935
ISBN 0-06-066318-9

83 84 85 86 87 10 9 8 7 6 5 4 3 2 1

*To all who bear witness to the presence of
the suffering Christ in Latin America*

CONTENTS

Acknowledgments
xi

INTRODUCTION
In Search of a Vocation
xiii

1.
OCTOBER
The Lord of the Miracles
1

2.
NOVEMBER
New Faces and Voices
23

3.
DECEMBER
A Land of Martyrs
61

4.
JANUARY
In Pablo and Sophia's House
97

5.
FEBRUARY
An Inner and Outer Struggle
127

6.
MARCH
The Outlines of a Vision
157

CONCLUSION
A Call to Be Grateful
187

Acknowledgments

This journal would never have been written without the generous hospitality and skillful assistance of many friends in Latin
America. Therefore my gratitude extends first to my many hosts.
Pete Byrne, the Superior of the Maryknoll fathers in Peru, was the
first to greet me when I came to Latin America. His faithful friendship became the context for many enriching experiences. In the
months to follow, many other members of the Maryknoll community offered me a warm welcome, especially Alex Walsh, Bill
McCarthy, Pete Ruggere, Tom Burns, and Charles Murray. They
made me feel at home in the Maryknoll Center house in Lima and
let me become part of their ministry in Ciudad de Dios. I am
especially grateful to Pablo and Sophia Oscco-Moreno for letting
me live with their family during my time in the parish.

My stay at the language institute in Bolivia would not have been
such a good experience without the great care and attention that
I received from the director, Gerry McCrane. Even if I had not
learned much Spanish, just coming to know him as a friend would
have made the trip worthwhile. I am also deeply grateful to Nancy
and Rodolfo Quiroga, who made me a true member of their family
during my two months in their home in Cochabamba. I fondly
remember their kindness and great patience in correcting my mistakes in Spanish.

Two dear friends, Fran Kersjes in Bolivia and Anne Marie
Tamariz in Peru, deserve a special word of thanks. They typed and
retyped the text as it was first written, making it possible for me
to send it to friends who wanted to know how things were going.
It was a joy to work with them.

This journal would never have been published without the
dedicated help of friends in the United States. I owe a deep grati-

tude to Bobby Massie, who spent many hours, days, and weeks editing the manuscript, suggesting cuts and changes, and helping me to separate the wheat from the chaff. His personal interest and his many words of encouragement have been essential for the progress of this project. Phil Zaeder and Peggy Schreiner generously offered their time and talents when the text needed a final critical reading. For their countless literary suggestions I am very grateful. I also want to say thanks to Richard Alan White, Robert Durback, and Fred Bratman for their insightful criticisms. Mabel Treadwell, June Hagan, and Carol Plantinga did much of the hard administrative and secretarial work during the last stages of this journal. Their generous help in sending the text to different readers and in typing and retyping it was indispensable. I cannot say "thanks" to them often enough.

John Shopp, my editor at Harper & Row, has been a great support all along the way. His personal interest in this journal and his great availability in discussing even minute details have been a real source of encouragement to me.

Finally, I want to say thanks to Joseph Núñez. He gave this journal its title and, by so doing, helped me see its main theme more clearly than ever before. When he said, "Why don't you call it *Gracias*—isn't that what you heard and said most of all?" I knew that he had made me aware of the main experience of my journey to Latin America.

Thus I can say to all who are mentioned in this journal, to all who helped it to be written and published, and to all who stand around it without being mentioned by name: *Gracias a Dios, gracias a ustedes, muchísimas gracias.*

INTRODUCTION

In Search of a Vocation

This journal is the personal report of my six-month sojourn in Bolivia and Peru. I wrote it in an attempt to capture the countless impressions, feelings, and ideas that filled my mind and heart day after day. It speaks about new places and people, about new insights and perspectives, and about new joys and anxieties. But the question that runs through all its pages and binds the many varied fragments together is: "Does God call me to live and work in Latin America in the years to come?" This vocational question has guided me in the selection of issues to comment upon, it has directed me in my observations, and it has deeply influenced my responses to what I have seen and heard. This journal, therefore, is neither a travel diary, nor an analysis of Latin American conditions, nor a critical study of political and religious movements. Even though I often mention interesting sights, describe distressing living conditions, and comment on the impact of political and religious currents, I do not claim more expertise than the expertise that comes from an honest search for a new vocation. This journal records a six-month journey toward discernment. In the midst of all the travels, language studies, conversations, and encounters, I tried to discern God's voice; and in the midst of the great variety of my inner responses, I tried to find the way to be obedient to that voice.

The question: "Does God call me to Latin America?" was not a new question for me. From the day I left Holland to teach pastoral theology at Yale Divinity School, I had been wondering about the connection between the northern and the southern parts of the American continent. Somehow I felt that teaching future ministers in the United States about God's mysterious work with people could not be done unless the word "people" included the millions of Spanish- and Portuguese-speaking human beings whose destiny is intimately linked with that of their English-speaking brothers and sisters. Somehow, I knew that God's voice could not be heard unless it would include the voices of the men, women, and children of Latin America. With this "knowledge," I made short visits to Mexico, Chile, and Paraguay, and took some language training in Bolivia. Although these excursions led only to piecemeal involvements and limited commitments, they deepened my conviction about the spiritual unity of the American continent.

Finally, after ten years, I felt free enough to confront directly the question that had haunted me for so long. I left the Divinity School, moved in temporarily with my Trappist friends at the Abbey of the Genesee in upstate New York, and started to prepare myself for a more systematic discernment of a possible vocation in Latin America. Meanwhile, the Maryknoll fathers in Peru had invited me to make Peru the center of my activities. They suggested, however, that I first go to Bolivia for some additional language training. Thus, in October 1981, I flew to Peru to get to know my Maryknoll hosts and from there to Cochabamba, Bolivia, for a three-month course designed to improve my Spanish. In January 1982, I returned to Peru for three months of orientation "in the field." It is these six months, from October 1981 to March 1982, that this journal records. In it, I tried to impose some order on the myriad experiences that were part of this journey. But, most of all, I have tried to find an answer to the question: "Does God call me to live and work in Latin America in the years to come?"

I am very glad that I can share this search for a new vocation with others, because I know that all who love God strive constantly to hear his voice more clearly. I therefore hope that telling my story will offer encouragement to others to tell theirs.

1.

OCTOBER

The Lord of the Miracles

Sunday, October 18
Lima, Peru

Thanks be to God for bringing me here. The closer I came to the day of departure, the more convinced I was that going to Latin America was indeed the thing to do. Off and on the thought occurred to me that I was not ready for this change. I felt too tired, too preoccupied with personal struggles, too restless, too busy, too unprepared. But as the day of departure drew closer, I felt a growing sense of call. What had seemed little more than an adventure now presented itself as a vocation.

I left the Abbey of the Genesee in upstate New York on Sunday, October 11, for a one-week visit to Yale Divinity School in New Haven, where I had taught for ten years. It proved to be an important week, in which all the contacts, discussions, prayers, and celebrations helped me to listen more carefully to God's call, to let go of what was past, and to look forward to a totally new ministry. It seems paradoxical, but the expressions of friendship at Yale of former students and colleagues, and the deep personal conversations, gave me a profound sense of mission. I realized that I was not going just because it seemed like a good idea, but because those who love me most sent me on my way with affection, support, and prayers. The more I realized that I was truly loved, the more I felt the inner freedom to go in peace and to let all inner debate about motivation subside.

The Eucharistic celebration on Friday afternoon meant more to me than I can express in words. I had a strong sense of community, and an awareness that this community will stay with me wherever I go. The Lord himself brought us together and has made it clear to us that we are One in him and that this unity will allow us to

1

be free, courageous, and full of hope. Whatever my experience in Latin America will bring to me, it will be part of a body formed in love and it will reverberate in all its members. The Body and Blood of our Lord Jesus Christ are indeed food for eternal life, a life that liberates us to live without fear and to travel without apprehension.

John Vesey drove me to the airport. He had come from Brooklyn to spend the last day in New Haven with me to help me pack. Our friendship started in Bolivia in the summer of 1972, when I was there for language training, and we have stayed in touch ever since. Having just returned from a seven-year ministry in Paraguay, he expressed his enthusiasm for my decision to return to Bolivia for more training and to join the Maryknoll fathers in Peru. His strong sense of God's guidance in our lives and his deep awareness of the beauty of the Divine in the midst of this dark world convinced me more than ever that it was good to go.

Monday, October 19

On the airplane to Lima, I spoke with the woman next to me. She told me that she was returning home with her mother, who had undergone three operations in the United States. "Is your mother better now?" I asked. "Oh yes, she is totally cured," she said with fervent conviction, "and the whole family is waiting at the airport to welcome her home." After a few minutes of silence, she wanted to know my reasons for going to Peru. When I told her that I was a priest planning to work with the Maryknoll missioners, her face changed dramatically. She leaned over to me, grabbed my hand, and whispered in an agonized way: "Oh Father, mother has cancer and there is little hope for her."

The first thing I learned about Peruvians was that they have an unlimited trust in priests. Even though the Church certainly has not earned such unconditional respect during the last centuries, the people of Peru give their confidence to their priests without hesitation. This impression was strongly affirmed on Sunday morning, when I found myself in the huge crowd on the Plaza de Armas, welcoming the procession of *el Señor de los milagros* (the Lord of the Miracles). As soon as the bystanders realized that I was a priest, they let go of their inhibitions, handed me their children to lift above the crowds, and told me about their joys and sorrows.

Peru: from the moment I entered it, I felt a deep love for this country. I do not know why. I did not feel this when I went to Chile or Bolivia in the past. But looking at the busy streets of Lima, the dark open faces and the lively gestures, I felt embraced by a loving people in a way I had not known before. Walking through the busy streets, looking at the men, women, and children in their penitential dress—purple habits with white cords—and sensing the gentle spirit of forgiveness, I had the strange emotion of home-coming. "This is where I belong. This is where I must be. This is where I will be for a very long time. This is home." Everything seemed easy. Thousands of people, but no pressing crowds; count-less voices, but no shouts or cries; a multitude of faces, but no anger or frustration. I had never experienced this before. The obvious explanation is that I saw Peru for the first time on the feast day of the Lord of the Miracles, a day celebrated with a procession characterized by repentance and quiet prayer. But for me it was a day of comfort and consolation, a day on which the decision to come to this country was affirmed.

I felt as though the crowds of Lima were embracing me and showering me with the affection I had missed during the past months. It seemed as if the whispering crowds, the gentle move-ments of the bearers of the picture of the Lord of the Miracles, and the uninhibited smiles of the children all said to me: "Do not be afraid, the Lord loves all of us . . . you too."

Yes, I saw the Lord! How strange was that first day in Lima. In the central square, with its many balconies, thousands of people had gathered. On one balcony, president Fernando Belaúnde Terry stood waiting to pay homage to the Christ being carried into his presence. On another, the mayor was ready to hand the key of the city to the Lord of the Miracles; and on a third bal-cony, the church dignitaries stood to bless the image of the Cru-cified. Who was bowing to whom? Who was using whom? Who was trying to win votes, admiration, or sympathy? Who knows? But the people applauded the One whom they trusted and left the president, the mayor, and the bishops to their own specula-tions. New bouquets of flowers were continually brought to the platform on which the Image of Christ slowly moved through the crowds. When I lifted up a little Peruvian girl and showed her the Lord of the Miracles, I felt that the Lord and the little girl were both telling me the same story: presidents, mayors, and bishops come and go, but our God continues to enter our lives and to invite children to climb on the shoulders of adults and recognize him.

On the evening of this first day in Peru, I had the sensation that I had been here for a long time and that all that I had heard and seen had a deep and old familiarity. Everything whispered, "Welcome home, my friend."

Tuesday, October 20

It took only a few hours to be immersed in the real questions. Monsignor Alberto Koenigsknecht introduced me to them without knowing he was doing so. Alberto, a Maryknoller, is the prelate of the diocese of Juli in the Altiplano. He is staying at the Maryknoll Center house in Lima to organize a day of prayer to protest the attacks against the Christian community in his prelature. On August 15, the Institute for Rural Education was ransacked. On September 19, dynamite exploded in the entrance of Alberto's home and a note was found with a death threat.

Alberto was careful in his explanation. "We do not know who did it and why it was done, but it certainly was well planned." In August 1979, a pastoral week was held in the diocese of Juli. This meeting showed a strong and unwavering commitment to the poor and the oppressed. The final text says: "We decide to commit ourselves to the poor, that is, to those who form the oppressed class, those who depend on their work but do not have the means to live a dignified life, since they are exploited by others who deny them their rights." These are very strong words when spoken or written in and about Peru, and it certainly is possible that the recent attacks and death threat are among the responses.

Alberto spoke to the underminister of justice, but received little support. An investigation was promised, but nothing happened. And now it is the Church's turn to respond. In a few weeks, on November fifteenth, Christians of Peru will be called to Juli to express solidarity with the poor and to give a clear sign that attacks and death threats are not going to change the chosen direction. Alberto realized that he was taking a risk, but he felt that he had to do it. Gustavo Gutiérrez, the father of liberation theology, and his staff were consulted. It had become evident that a clear sign was needed to show the strength of the Church's commitment.

I sense that all of this might be just the beginning of a long road of suffering. Similar things have happened in El Salvador, similar things are happening in Guatemala, and the small rumblings in Peru seem to belong to that same awakening of the people of God in Latin America.

Wednesday, October 21

Pete Byrne, the superior of the Maryknoll fathers in Peru, drove me to the Ciudad de Dios (the City of God). "This is the parish where you will live and work when you come back from language school," he said with excitement. "You will love it. Now it all looks strange and unfamiliar to you, but it won't take long for you to feel part of the people here. They will love you and you will love them." Pete drove his car through the crowds gathering around the marketplace and took me to the Pamplona Alta section, where Maryknoll missioners Pete Ruggere, Tom Burns, and Larry Rich are living.

I was struck not only by the obvious poverty of the people, but also by their dignity. They care for what they own, and they manage to keep little gardens in the midst of this dry, sandy, and dusty place. Thousands of people live here—125,000—but there is space between houses as well as between people. The area is poor, very poor, but not depressing. It is full of visible problems, but not without hope.

Later in the day an elderly laywoman dressed as a nun—Maria is her name—told me about the beginning of the Ciudad de Dios. Ciudad de Dios was the result of a popular invasion on Christmas Eve 1954. Maria remembered that day with a sense of pride. She belonged to the founding fathers and mothers. On that Christmas night, thousands of people illegally occupied the barren land and immediately started to develop it. The government had no choice but to comply and eventually help, and now there is the City of God with countless brick houses, a large church, a school, and several medical posts.

The invasion of Ciudad de Dios was one of the first in a long series of similar invasions. Poverty and lack of land forced a constant migration from the countryside to the city. The Indian migrants first lived with relatives and friends; but when they became too numerous and desperate for a space and a livelihood, they organized themselves and seized the barren desert land surrounding the city. Today Lima has a large belt of "young towns," many of which are the result of these illegal land seizures.

Pamplona Alta, which belongs to the same parish, developed a few years after Ciudad de Dios was founded. From the many little shacks visible on the bare hills beyond Pamplona Alta, it is clear that invasions—although on a much smaller scale—are still taking place today.

Pete Ruggere welcomed me to the house where I would stay in January. It consists of brick walls, a cement floor, and a roof put together with pieces of wood, plastic, and straw. "It gets wet here when it rains," Pete observed, "but it seldom rains." We visited the neighbors: a husband, wife, and eleven children, all living in two rooms. There were lots of smiles, laughter, and affection, but I noticed exhaustion on the face of the mother. She carried a two-month-old baby in her arms while pointing to the one-and-a-half-year-old girl on the bed. I tried to get a smile from her, but found little response. Pete told me she was just diagnosed as having Down syndrome.

I spent the day visiting Maureen, a Dominican nurse, walking around the area, attending a mass during which the sick were anointed, talking to Sister Vivian, a Maryknoll doctor, and just wondering what it would be like to live here.

During the evening, I picked up some of Gustavo Gutiérrez's early writings. My visit to Ciudad de Dios makes his words sound very real. This, indeed, is a theology born out of solidarity with the people. The people speak about God and his Presence in ways I must slowly come to understand. It will take time, much time, but a willingness to learn is one thing I can bring here.

Before leaving for Bolivia, I would like to make some notes about Maryknoll and its role in Latin America. The first objective of the Maryknoll Society, as expressed by the General Chapter in 1979, is: "To recognize and elaborate a mission of spirituality which integrates community, prayer, a simple life-style, apostolic work, and commitment to the poor." I like the word "recognize." A true spirituality cannot be constructed, built, or put together; it has to be recognized in the daily life of people who search together to do God's will in the world.

I am impressed by the documents written about Peru by the Maryknollers. Their socioeconomic, political, and religious analyses are well-documented, clearly explained, and skillfully integrated into their self-understanding as missioners. A few simple facts are worth remembering. The present population of Peru is about 17 million (54% mestizo [mixed Indian and white], 33% Indian, 13% white). The main perspective of the Maryknoll missioners in Peru is summarized well in the following quote:

> The vast majority of Peruvians are classified as poor or "lower class" workers, campesinos or unemployed. This class is distinguished by race: it is composed of Indians, blacks and mestizos. It is dominated by the "upper class" and it is considered inferior. The Peruvian "middle-class" is composed of professionals who are generally either white or mestizos and though economically and politically it is gaining strength, it is numerically small and no rival to the power of the "upper class." The "upper class" is white and though minute it controls the wealth and the political power of the country.
>
> One fourth of one percent of the population receives more than 33% of all income in the country. The predominant social dynamic in Peru is the structural oppression and domination of the "lower class" and the emerging resistance of the poor to this domination (*Peru Regional Directory,* 1980, p. 3).

This is the context of the work of the Maryknoll Society, and the background against which its commitment to the poor needs to be understood. There are about forty-eight people directly connected with the work of the Maryknoll fathers in Peru (priests, associate priests, brothers, and lay missioners). Their activities are varied: parish work, religious training and formation, counseling, teaching, small group work, publishing, research, and so forth. They work in the Juli Prelature, in Arequipa, Huacho, and Lima. Maryknoll came to Peru in 1943, and has focused in different ways on the development of the local church. "To create self-directing, self-sustaining, and self-propagating Christian Communities captures the thrust of Maryknoll work in Peru from the beginning but the manner and emphasis have changed over the years."

The change in "manner and emphasis" of the missionary activities of Maryknoll over the years is of crucial importance. One Maryknoll priest, Ralph Davila, remarked during dinner: "It is the change from selling pearls to hunting for the treasure." Indeed, not too long ago, the main task was seen as selling the pearls of good news to the poor and ignorant people. Now a radically new perspective dominates the Maryknoll activities: to search with the poor for the treasure hidden in the ground on which they stand. It is this shift from spiritual colonialism to solidarity in servanthood that explains the style of life, the way of speech, the kind of literature, and the overall mood that I have become part of during the last few days.

I really feel that I am welcome here, not just as a guest who can learn a lot from Maryknoll, but also as someone from whom some contribution is expected. At this moment I cannot think of myself as someone who has anything to offer—I feel like someone surrounded by experts—but I am willing to live with the supposition that he who truly receives also gives. It is encouraging to feel part of a true community of apostolic love and fervor so soon. I now am ready to go to Bolivia for language training, because I now know that I will be welcome here when I return.

Thursday, October 22
Cochabamba, Bolivia

Today I flew from Lima to La Paz and from La Paz to Cochabamba. It was a magnificent flight over Lake Titicaca and over the wild and desolate mountain ranges of Bolivia. In the plane I talked with Henry Perry, a surgeon from Duke University, who hopes to set up elaborate health services in Achacachi, and with a young woman from San Francisco, who is dedicated to studying the intricate weaving techniques of the Indians in Ecuador, Peru, and Bolivia.

Warm summer weather engulfed me when I stepped off the plane, and the taxi ride to the Instituto de Idiomas, the language school, showed me clearly that Cochabamba is, indeed, the garden city of Bolivia. The great wealth of flowers reminded me that it is spring here, and that it will be midsummer when December comes.

Gerald McCrane, the director of the institute, welcomed me warmly and invited me to look with some of the students of the institute at a videotape of a CBS report on El Salvador. And thus, staying in one of the most lovely towns of Latin America, I am reminded that violence, oppression, persecution, torture, and indescribable human misery are all around. The film showed the civil war in El Salvador in gruesome detail. The Bolivians who watched it with us remarked that similar things were happening here.

Latin America: impressive wealth and degrading poverty, splendid flowers and dusty broken roads, loving people and cruel torturers, smiling children and soldiers who kill. It is here that we have to hunt for God's treasure.

I pray that my stay in Bolivia will teach me much more than Spanish.

Friday, October 23

Today was a day of getting used to my new environment. This seems easy: friendly people, beautiful gardens, and a smoothly run school. But when I reflect on what is going on underneath this comfortable exterior, I realize that I probably will never get used to my new world.

Chris Hedges, a Harvard Divinity School student, told me about the drug traffic in Bolivia. A Maryknoller visiting the institute explained to me how the military pushes Bolivia into bankruptcy, creates terror all through the country, and imprisons, kills, and tortures at random.

At lunch I met the Archbishop of La Paz, Monsignor Manrique. A short man with dark, Indian features, he impresses me as a simple and humble person. As the many stories indicate, he is one of the few people who dare to resist the regime. His faith gives him the moral power to speak out forcefully against the oppression of his people. In 1978, twelve hundred people staged a three-week-long hunger strike to reinforce their demands for an amnesty for all political prisoners and exiles. The government of General Banzer was forced to capitulate, but only after Manrique threatened to close all the churches of the diocese. He once said to the military: "You play tigers in La Paz in front of unarmed citizens, but you are cowards on the borders when you are facing the Chileans. You haven't won one war yet." Archbishop Manrique is undoubtedly one of the most courageous Christian leaders in Latin America, deeply loved by the miners and workers of Bolivia for his consistent demands for justice. I asked him if there were any priests in prison. He said: "At this moment, no. The human rights committee of the UN is coming to Bolivia today, and that helps."

Bolivia desperately wants recognition from the United States as a way to prevent total economic chaos. The Reagan administration requires an end to the drug traffic as a condition for recognition. The military, however, is so heavily involved in this illegal business, which brings in more money than all the mining industries put together, that any significant action can hardly be expected. So now there are some sporadic antidrug actions in the Beni (Bolivian lowlands). The victims—as always—are not the big cocaine traffickers, but some innocent *campesinos.* Meanwhile, the United States government seems to be placated with these gestures, and the newspapers expect a speedy recognition from Reagan.

I guess it is better not to get used to my new environment too soon.

Saturday, October 24

Although it is only a week ago that I came to Latin America, I have been here for a long time. The many new things I saw and heard during the last seven days must have intensified my mental activity. At the same time, I have had more time for myself than I have had for a long time—more time to pray, more time to read, more time to talk to people, more time to relax and just look around.

Today was a day in which prayer was uppermost on my mind. Last night the Franciscan priest, Justus Wirth, said in his reflection on the Gospel that the new commitment to the poor and the new emphasis on prayer were both signs of the action of the Holy Spirit in our time. When he said this, I suddenly realized that, indeed, prayer and work with the poor belong together and that the need to pray had grown in me ever since I have been confronted with the oppression and exploitation of the poor in Peru and Bolivia.

The several times I awoke last night, I found myself saying: "Lord, give me a true desire to pray"; and today I found it easier than before just to sit in the presence of God and listen quietly. I am grateful for this experience, and I am slowly becoming aware that something new is happening in me.

One image has been with me ever since I saw Pamplona Alta in Lima. It is the image of living as a hermit in the midst of the poor. That image must have been vague and subconscious, since I never wrote or spoke about it. But when a visiting priest from the St. Louis, Missouri, diocese said to me: "I am living in a poor section of La Paz as a hermit among the people," I immediately understood him. Yes—indeed, just to pray for, with, and among the poor spoke to me as a true missionary vocation. Wouldn't that be an authentic way of entering into solidarity with those who have nothing to lose?

True prayer always includes becoming poor. When we pray we stand naked and vulnerable in front of Our Lord and show him our true condition. If one were to do this not just for oneself, but in the name of the thousands of surrounding poor people, wouldn't that be "mission" in the true sense of being sent into the world as Jesus himself was sent into the world? To lift up your hands to the Lord and show him the hungry children who play on the dusty streets, the tired women who carry their babies on their backs to the marketplace, the men who try to forget their misery by drinking too much beer on the weekends, the jobless teenagers and the homeless squatters, together with their laughter, friendly gestures, and gentle words—wouldn't that be true service? If God really exists, if he truly cares, if he never leaves his people alone, who is there to remind him of his promises? Who is there to cry out: "How long will you frown on your people's plea? . . . Turn again, we implore, look down from heaven and see. Visit this vine and protect it, the vine your right hand has planted. . . . Let your face shine on us, and we shall be saved" (Ps. 80)? I feel that in a world rushing to the abyss, the need for calling God to the task, for challenging him to make his love felt among the poor, is more urgent than ever.

There were many wars, conflicts, and much poverty and misery in the thirteenth century, but we do not remember the political struggles and the socioeconomic events of that century. We remember one man who lived in the midst of it and prayed, prayed, and prayed until his hands and feet were pierced with the wounds of Christ himself. Who will be the St. Francis of our age? Many are asking themselves this question again. Who will lift up the world of today to God and plead for his mercy? Why does God still allow this world to continue? Because of Ronald Reagan, Begin, Brezhnev, Thatcher, Marcos, Belaúnde, or Torrelio? Or perhaps because of the few hermits hidden in the forests of Russia, on the roofs of New York City, and in the *favelas* of Brazil, Peru, and Bolivia? When the Lord looks down on us, what does he see?

He sees his son Jesus in the faces of the few who continue to cry out in the valley of tears. For Jesus' sake he will save us from total destruction.

Prayer is the ongoing cry of the incarnate Lord to the loving God. It is eternity in the midst of mortality, it is life among death, hope in the midst of despair, true promise surrounded by lies. Prayer brings love alive among us. So let us pray unceasingly.

Sunday, October 25

Donald Stoker, an English priest, said to me last night: "Did you notice the night sounds here? When you go to bed you hear the bullfrogs croak. When you wake up at two in the night you hear the dogs bark. When you wake up at four you hear the cocks crow, and when you get up at six you hear the birds sing." Indeed, there are no silent nights in Bolivia. And during the day the voices of playing children join the birds in their chatter. All these sounds come together to form a single unceasing prayer to the Creator, a prayer not of thoughts and words but of sounds and life. How sad it is that thinking often makes prayers cease.

Monday, October 26

Chris Hedges gave me an article to read called, "Up to Our Steeple in Politics." It is written by Will D. Campbell and James Holloway and published in *Christianity and Crisis* on March 3, 1969. In it, the authors explore the issue of exactly how far the Church can become involved in politics without being corrupted by it, how far one can go into the world of Caesar before one loses sight of God.

The questions Campbell and Holloway raise are as important for the Latin American upheavals as they were for the civil rights movement in the United States, about which they were writing. Will we ever know whether we are living witnesses to the light or serving the prince of darkness? That is the question for the four priests who participated in the revolution in Nicaragua and are now members of the new Sandinista cabinet. That, too, is the question for Christians active in agrarian reform, in the development of cooperatives for the *campesinos,* and in programs for better health and better housing.

The Christian is called to live in the world without being of it.

But how do we know whether we are just in it, or also of it? My feeling is that every Christian who is serious about his or her vocation has to face this question at some point.

How, then, are we to find the right answer for ourselves? Here we are called to discern carefully the movements of God's Spirit in our lives. Discernment remains our lifelong task. I can see no other way for discernment than a life in the Spirit, a life of unceasing prayer and contemplation, a life of deep communion with the Spirit of God. Such a life will slowly develop in us an inner sensitivity, enabling us to distinguish between the law of the flesh and the law of the spirit. We certainly will make constant errors and seldom have the purity of heart required to make the right decisions. We may never know whether we are giving to Caesar what belongs to God. But when we continuously try to live in the Spirit, we at least shall be willing to confess our weakness and ask for forgiveness every time we find ourselves again in the service of Baal.

Tuesday, October 27

This is my second day of language training, frustrating and exhilarating at the same time. It is frustrating, since I make the same mistakes I made nine years ago and continue to have the feeling that I should be much more advanced after the many weeks and months I have worked on Spanish in the past. There are frequent moments during which I say to myself: "I will never master this language." But the same experience is also refreshing. I can be a student again. I can spend many hours doing simple exercises that often appear as little puzzles, and I can be with other people who go through the same frustrations as I do. The teachers are dedicated and are always in a good mood and willing to help inside and outside of classes. The institute is equipped with the best possible facilities and everything is well organized. I can hardly think of a better place to learn a new language.

During the sixties, I spent two weeks in Madrid and a month in Cuernavaca with the conviction that Spanish was essential for my future work. But I never practiced it outside the formal training periods. Then I came here in the summer of 1972 and gave it another try. Again my acquired knowledge slipped away and now —nine years later—I feel that again I am beginning from scratch.

As I reflect on this fragmented approach to mastering Spanish, I can only say that I never gave up the deep conviction that I must learn it somehow, sometime. I never have been able fully to explain this conviction to myself or to anyone else. But the urge always was there and still is there; my desire to know Spanish and to know it well is as strong as ever. Why? I don't know. I hope that I will know before I die. There must be a meaning to such a strange passion!

I just read Paul Blustein's article about the Maryknollers in Peru. It gave me a strong sense of *déjà vu.* Blustein speaks about his encounter with Pete Ruggere and about his visit to Pete's neighbors:

> On a urine-soaked bed near the entrance lies an infant girl who, Father Ruggere says, suffers from malnutrition and almost certainly won't live beyond her fifth birthday. When the priest swoops the baby into his arms, gurgling endearments in Spanish, the child neither laughs nor cries, but merely gazes blankly at him through filmy brown eyes . . . (*Wall Street Journal,* August 14, 1981).

When I read this I saw it all over again, and realized that he was speaking about my future neighbors. The article is a masterful piece of reporting and one of the most balanced descriptions of the Maryknoll work I have read or heard.

Wednesday, October 28

This afternoon at three o'clock, my sister called from Holland to tell me that my sister-in-law had given birth to a daughter who was diagnosed as suffering from Down syndrome. A week ago I wrote about having seen a Down syndrome child in the house of Pete Ruggere's neighbors; yesterday I read about that child in the *Wall Street Journal;* today I have a niece who suffers from the same disease. I called Holland and talked to Heiltjen, my sister-in-law. The baby, she told me, had been born five hours previously, and the doctors had told her immediately about the child's handicap. "With Laura, our lives will be very different from now on," she said. My brother Laurent was not in the hospital when I called, but my sister as well as Heiltjen told me how distressed he was.

I still find it hard to appropriate this news. I cannot think about much else than this little child who will become the center of my brother and my sister-in-law's lives and will bring them into a world of which they have never dreamt. It will be a world of constant care and attention; a world of very small progressions; a world of new feelings, emotions, and thoughts; a world of affections that come from places invisible in "normal" people.

I know that Laurent and Heiltjen's love is being tested, not only their love for their new child but even more their love for each other and for their two-year-old daughter Sarah. I pray tonight for them that they will be able to grow in love because of Laura, and that they will discover in her the presence of God in their lives.

Laura is going to be important for all of us in the family. We have never had a "weak" person among us. We all are hardworking, ambitious, and successful people who seldom have had to experience powerlessness. Now Laura enters and tells us a totally new story, a story of weakness, brokenness, vulnerability, and total dependency. Laura, who always will be a child, will teach us the way of Christ as no one will ever be able to do.

I hope and pray that I can be of some support to Laurent and Heiltjen in their long journey with Laura, and that Laura will bring all of us closer together and closer to God.

Thursday, October 29

Tonight the Dominican priest, John Risley, spoke at the institute about the Puebla Documents. These are the public statements that were the result of the 1978 Latin American Bishops' Conference in Puebla, Mexico. The main point he made was that the Church had made a definite choice for the poor. Thus, he said, Puebla brought good news for the poor but bad news for those who hold power and do not want to give it up. The lively discussion that followed revealed various opinions about the implications of such a "preferential option" and about the theology of liberation in general.

One thought hit me in the midst of all the viewpoints, opinions, and ideas that were expressed. It was the thought that the poor themselves are the best evangelizers. I have already met a few very simple people here who revealed to me God's presence in life in a way nobody else could. During breakfast this morning I spoke to Lucha, one of the maids working in the institute. We did not speak about God or religion, but her smile, her kindness, the way she corrected my Spanish, and her stories about her children created a sense of spiritual jealousy in me. I kept thinking: "I wish I had the purity of heart of this woman, I wish I could be as simple, open, and gentle as she is. I wish I could be as in touch." But then I realized that maybe even she didn't know what she was giving me. Thus my ministry to her is to allow her to show me the Lord and gratefully to acknowledge what I am receiving.

True liberation is freeing people from the bonds that have prevented them from giving their gifts to others. This is not only true for individual people but also—particularly—for ethnic groups. What does mission to the Indians really mean? Isn't it foremost to discover with them their own deep religiosity, their profound faith in God's active presence in history, and their understanding of the mystery of nature that surrounds them?

It is hard for me to accept that the best I can do is probably not to give but to receive. By receiving in a true and open way, those who give to me can become aware of their own gifts. After all, we come to recognize our own gifts in the eyes of those who receive them gratefully. Gratitude thus becomes the central virtue of a missionary. And what else is the Eucharistic life than a life of gratitude?

Friday, October 30

Today Gerry McCrane, the director of the language school, gave a presentation to the newcomers. In his gentle and pastoral way he offered us an opportunity to share our struggles in adapting ourselves to a new culture.

One theme that came up was the re-emergence of long-forgotten conflicts. In displacing ourselves into a new and unfamiliar milieu, old, unresolved conflicts often start asking for attention. When our traditional defense systems no longer are available and we are not able to control our own world, we often find ourselves experiencing again the feelings of childhood. The inability to express ourselves in words as well as the realization that everyone around us seems to understand life much better than we do, puts us in a situation quite similar to that of a child who has to struggle through a world of adults.

This return to childhood emotions and behavior could be a real opportunity for mental and spiritual growth. Most of the psychotherapies I have been exposed to were attempts to help me relive those times when immature ways of coping with stress found their origin. Once I could re-encounter the experience that led me to choose a primitive coping device, I was also able to choose a more mature response. Thus I could let go of behavior that was the source of my suffering. A good psychotherapist is a person who creates the environment in which such mature behavioral choices can be made.

Going to a different culture, in which I find myself again like a child, can become a true psychotherapeutic opportunity. Not everyone is in the position or has the support to use such an opportunity. I have seen much self-righteous, condescending, and even offensive behavior by foreigners towards the people in their host country. Remarks about the laziness, stupidity, and disorganization of Peruvians or Bolivians usually say a lot more about the one who makes such remarks than about Peruvians or Bolivians. Most of the labels by which we pigeonhole people are ways to cope with our own anxiety and insecurity. Many people who suddenly find themselves in a totally unfamiliar milieu decide quickly to label that which is strange to them instead of confronting their own fears and vulnerabilities.

But we can also use the new opportunity for our own healing. When we walk around in a strange milieu, speaking the language haltingly, and feeling out of control and like fools, we can come in touch with a part of ourselves that usually remains hidden behind the thick walls of our defenses. We can come to experience our basic vulnerability, our need for others, our deep-seated feelings of ignorance and inadequacy, and our fundamental dependency. Instead of running away from these scary feelings, we can live through them together and learn that our true value as human beings has its seat far beyond our competence and accomplishments.

One of the most rewarding aspects of living in a strange land is the experience of being loved not for what we can do, but for who we are. When we become aware that our stuttering, failing, vulnerable selves are loved even when we hardly progress, we can let go of our compulsion to prove ourselves and be free to live with others in a fellowship of the weak. That is true healing.

This psychological perspective on culture shock can open up for us a new understanding of God's grace and our vocation to live graceful lives. In the presence of God, we are totally naked, broken, sinful, and dependent, and we realize that we can do nothing, absolutely nothing, without him. When we are willing to confess our true condition, God will embrace us with his love, a love so deep, intimate, and strong that it enables us to make all things new. I am convinced that, for Christians, culture shock can be an opportunity not only for psychological healing but also for conversion.

What moves me most in reflecting on these opportunities is that they lead us to the heart of ministry and mission. The more I think about the meaning of living and acting in the name of Christ, the more I realize that what I have to offer to others is not my intelligence, skill, power, influence, or connections, but my own human brokenness through which the love of God can manifest itself. The celebrant in Leonard Bernstein's *Mass* says: "Glass shines brighter when it's broken. . . . I never noticed that." This, to me, is what ministry and mission are all about. Ministry is entering with our human brokenness into communion with others and speaking a word of hope. This hope is not based on any power to solve the problems of those with whom we live, but on the love of God, which becomes visible when we let go of our fears of being out of control and enter into his presence in a shared confession of weakness.

This is a hard vocation. It goes against the grain of our need for self-affirmation, self-fulfillment, and self-realization. It is a call to true humility. I, therefore, think that for those who are pulled away from their familiar surroundings and brought into a strange land where they feel again like babies, the Lord offers a unique chance not only for personal conversion but also for an authentic ministry.

Saturday, October 31

During the last few days, I have been thinking about the significance of gratitude in mission work. Gratitude is becoming increasingly important for those who want to bring the good news of the Kingdom to others. For a long time, the predominant attitude of the missioners was that they had to bring the knowledge of the Gospel to poor, ignorant people and thus offer light in their darkness. In such a view, there is not much room for gratitude.

As the missionary attitude changed, however, and more and more missioners came to see their task as helping others to recognize their own God-given talents, and thus to claim the good news for themselves, gratitude became much more than an occasional "thanks be to God." Gratitude is the attitude which enables us to receive the hidden gifts of those we want to serve and to make these gifts visible to the community as a source of celebration.

There is little doubt that jealousy, rivalry, anger, and resentment dominate our society much more than gratitude. Most people are afraid to make themselves available to others. They fear that they will be manipulated and exploited. They choose the safe way of hiding themselves and thus remaining unnoticed and anonymous. But in such a milieu of suspicion and fear, no community can develop and no good news can become visible.

True missioners are people who are hunting for the Divine treasure hidden in the heart of the people to whom they want to make the Good News known. They always expect to see the beauty and truth of God shining through those with whom they live and work.

The great paradox of ministry, therefore, is that we minister above all with our weakness, a weakness that invites us to receive from those to whom we go. The more in touch we are with our own need for healing and salvation, the more open we are to receive in gratitude what others have to offer us. The true skill of ministry is to help fearful and often oppressed men and women become aware of their own gifts, by receiving them in gratitude. In that sense, ministry becomes the skill of active dependency: willing to be dependent on what others have to give but often do not realize they have. By receiving in gratitude what we have helped others to discover in themselves, we enable them to claim for themselves full membership in the human and Christian community. Only those who truly believe that they have something to offer can experience themselves as spiritually adult. As long as someone feels that he or she is only an object of someone else's generosity, no dialogue, no mutuality, and no authentic community can exist.

As ministers, we share with all other human beings—especially those who have elaborate education and training—the desire to be in control, to tell others what to do and how to think. But if we want to follow Christ and "have his mind," we are called to empty ourselves of these privileges and become servants of the people. True servants depend on those whom they serve. They are called to live lives in which others guide them, often to places they would rather not go.

In different ways, these thoughts have been part of my understanding of ministry for over a decade. But here in Bolivia, in a different milieu, these ideas have taken deeper root; I no longer consider them romantic or sentimental. There is a danger of interpreting these thoughts about gratitude as a requirement to have certain concrete emotions towards others. But how can I feel grateful when I see so many poor, tired, and often apathetic people? My first response is: "How can I give them food, a house, an education, and a job?"

What then is it that we do receive in ministry? Is it the hidden insights and skills of those to whom we want to bear witness? Maybe so . . . but that can never be the true source of our own growth. Seeing how a person slowly becomes aware of his or her own capacities might make us happy for awhile, but that is not enough for a grateful life. A grateful life is a life in which we come to see that the Lord himself is the gift. The mystery of ministry is that the Lord is to be found where we minister. That is what Jesus tells us when he says: "Insofar as you did this to one of the least of these brothers of mine, you did it to me" (Matt. 25:40). Our care for people thus becomes the way to meet the Lord. The more we give, help, support, guide, counsel, and visit, the more we receive, not just similar gifts, but the Lord himself. To go to the poor is to go to the Lord. Living this truth in our daily life makes it possible to care for people without conditions, without hesitation, without suspicion, or without the need for immediate rewards. With this sacred knowledge, we can avoid becoming burned out.

The goal of education and formation for the ministry is continually to recognize the Lord's voice, his face, and his touch in every person we meet. As long as we live, the Lord wants to reveal to us more of himself. As long as we minister, we can expect the Lord to make himself known to us in ways we have not yet experienced. God himself became flesh for us so that we would be able to receive him every time we find ourselves serving another human being.

The question, however, is not only what are we receiving, but who is the receiver? Is it just *I*, with my unique capacity to see or hear, while others remain blind and deaf? No, because to see or to hear God is not a human possibility. It is a divine sensitivity. It is the Spirit of God in us who gives us eyes to see and ears to hear, who allows us to see and hear God in every person we serve.

God is thus not only the gift, but also the receiver. Just as it is not we who pray, but the Spirit in us, so it is not we who receive but the Spirit in us.

Gratitude is not just a psychological disposition, but a virtue. Gratitude is an intimate participation in the Divine Life itself. The Spirit of God in us recognizes God in the world. The eyes and ears by which we can see God in others are in fact spiritual sensitivities that allow us to receive our neighbor as a messenger of God himself.

This theological perspective on gratitude makes it clear why it is so crucial that we pray: through prayer we become aware of the life of God within us and it is this God within us who allows us to recognize the God among us. When we have met our Lord in the silent intimacy of our prayer, then we will also meet him in the *campo,* in the market, and in the town square. But when we have not met him in the center of our own hearts, we cannot expect to meet him in the busyness of our daily lives. Gratitude is God receiving God in and through the human interaction of ministry. This viewpoint explains why true ministers, true missionaries, are always also contemplatives. Seeing God in the world and making him visible to each other is the core of ministry as well as the core of the contemplative life.

Today, Reformation Day, a group of North American Lutheran ministers is visiting the institute. They are traveling through Latin America in order to evaluate their mission work. They come with open minds and hearts. Their vision is very much in tune with the vision of Maryknoll, and their main question is: "How can we work together to make and fulfill our common call to evangelize the nations?"

I was invited to attend the meeting, and I felt part of an extremely important new form of ecumenism: cooperation in the missions between the Roman Catholic and the Lutheran communities. To set the tone, Gerry McCrane gave all of us the following words, written by a third world bishop for those who come as missioners to Latin America.

Walk with Us in Our Search

Help us discover our own riches; don't judge us poor because we lack what you have.

Help us discover our chains; don't judge us slaves by the type of shackles you wear.

Be patient with us as a people; don't judge us backward simply because we don't follow your stride.

Be patient with our pace; don't judge us lazy simply because we can't follow your tempo.

Be patient with our symbols; don't judge us ignorant because we can't read your signs.

Be with us and proclaim the richness of your life which you can share with us.

Be with us and be open to what we can give.

Be with us as a companion who walks with us—neither behind nor in front—in our search for life and ultimately for God!

These words not only point toward a contemporary missionary spirituality, but also offer a base for true ecumenism in Latin America. Because, whether we are Lutherans or Roman Catholics, we first of all must listen to the people to whom we come; it is they who will show us the way to Christian unity.

2.

N O V E M B E R

New Faces and Voices

Sunday, November 1, All Saints Day

This morning I went with Brian Clark, a journalist for the *Modesto* [California] *Bee,* and with Simon, a Redemptorist brother, to Mass in the Church of Santa Ana. The Dominican priest, Oscar Uzin, celebrated the Eucharist. In a simple, clear, and convincing way, he explained the meaning of All Saints Day: "We do not concentrate today on spiritual heroes, but on people who are saints by loving one another, caring for one another, forgiving one another in their normal, everyday lives. We are celebrating the saints among us who do not have haloes above their heads but who, formed and inspired by the gospel, can make the interest of others more important than their own."

I felt at home in this simple Sunday liturgy. The church was packed with people, young and old, men and women, Cochabambinos and foreigners. Everybody was attentive and many went to communion. It was easy to feel part of this celebration, and, as always in situations like this, I marvel at the universal appeal of the words of Our Lord.

Tonight I was looking at the new moon and the bright stars decorating the wide skies of Bolivia. The air was cool and pleasant. Ernie, an eighty-two-year-old man from Rhode Island, joined me. After a moment of silence, he said: "Nice climate here; if the government were the same, everything would be all right."

Monday, November 2, All Souls Day

Throughout Latin America, All Souls Day is a special feast, the day in which people pay tribute to and enter into communion with those who have died. The place where this celebration of the lasting bonds with the dead can be experienced is the cemetery.

For me, the day started quietly. I spent an hour in the early morning in silent prayer for my mother and all the family members and friends who had died over the last years. From that intimate center, I let the eyes of my mind wander into wider and wider circles. I first saw the many acquaintances in my own little world who are no longer with me, then I thought about the many whose deaths I had learned of through newspapers, radio, and television, and finally I saw the thousands and thousands who had lost their lives through hunger and violence and whose names would always remain unknown to me. Suddenly, I found myself surrounded by a crowd of people who had been cruelly snatched away from life without a prayer, a word of consolation, or even a kiss on the forehead. To all of these I was intimately linked— so intimately that their total freedom had come to depend more and more on this ongoing connection stretching out far beyond the boundary of death. Indeed, part of the meaning of life for the living is our opportunity to pray for the full liberation of those who died before us.

With these thoughts, I began a busy day, which included a visit to the doctor and four classes in Spanish. At 2:30 P.M. I was free to join some friends for a visit to the cemetery of Cochabamba. What I saw there I will never forget. Thousands of people were sitting and walking around the graves as though they were camping with their beloved ones who had died. All types of sounds were mingled together: the sound of boys praying aloud, the sound of a trumpet, the sound of friendly conversations, the sounds of laughter and tears. Was this a gigantic picnic, a massive wake, a city-wide prayer service, a feast, a reunion, a day of repentance, or a celebration of continuing brotherhood and sisterhood? It obviously was all of that and much, much more. Something became visible at that cemetery that defied our usual distinctions between sorrow and joy, mourning and feasting, eating and fasting, praying and playing, and, most of all, living and dying. The people who came together at the cemetery revealed a reality that cannot be grasped by any of the categories that we use to define our daily experiences.

One sad exception remained: the distinction between the rich and the poor. We entered the cemetery through a large gate inscribed with the words, *Fiat Voluntas Tua* ("Your Will Be Done");

but after having passed the large monumental graves and the huge walls with square niches, we soon found ourselves in an open field covered with small wooden crosses that marked the rudimentary graves of the poor. And when we left the official cemetery through a small gate in the back wall, we came upon a large sandy stretch of land where hundreds of people who could not pay for even the simplest spot had claimed a place where they could bury their relatives and visit them. Sister Jeri Cashman, who had lived in Cochabamba for quite some time, explained that after five years the bodies of the poor are removed and burned to make a place for others. A large pit in which you could see pieces of skulls and bones showed that this burning of the poor was a daily event.

Somehow, I felt much more at home in the open field than between the monuments and the walls with niches. Wherever we walked people looked at us with friendly smiles, as if they were grateful that we had come. They appeared to be at a party. Each grave was surrounded by people who had spread a blanket over the grave and covered it with food: bananas, oranges, and all forms of *urpo,* a special bread baked for this day. Often the centerpiece was a cake in the form of a man or woman, representing the one who was buried under the blanket. At one place I saw a large bread, standing up in the form of a man with uniform and gun, indicating that the family was mourning the death of a soldier. Sister Jeri explained: "The people bring all sorts of food to the graves, often the food their deceased relatives most liked, and then they have a meal with them and thus continue to stay in touch."

What caught my attention most of all were the praying boys. In pairs, ten- to twelve-year-old boys walked all over the cemetery with large white sacks over their shoulders. One of each couple had a small booklet. They went from grave to grave asking if the people would let them pray. When the answer was yes, they knelt down in front of the grave, one boy loudly reciting the litany printed in his booklet, the other responding even more loudly every ten seconds: "Let us praise the Lord in the Blessed Sacrament of the altar and the Virgin Mary conceived without original sin." It was clear that the boys had hardly any idea what they were saying, but their eyes were tightly closed and their hands devoutly folded. All over the cemetery the boys' voices sounded in a strangely pleasant rhythm that seemed to unite all that was happening into one great prayer. The members of the family themselves did not utter a word; that was the boys' task. After they had finished their booklet, the boys rose from their knees and opened their sacks to receive the pay for their prayers: a banana, a few cookies, a piece of cake, or whatever they could get. Then they went on to the next grave, while another couple of boys took their place. And so it went on the whole day. When the fruit and the bread had vanished from the blankets into the boys' sacks, fresh food was brought and put on the grave, often arranged in a decorative way.

At one place, I saw an old and inebriated man urging a family to let him pray for their dead. After some pleading, he received permission. He started to say an Our Father and a Hail Mary, but he was so drunk that he could hardly finish it. When he received only one cookie for his prayers, he said with some indignation in his voice: "Is that all?" The head of the family said "Yes," and signaled two boys to take over his poorly performed task. Having watched this scene for a while, I introduced myself to the family. When they heard I was a Dutch priest, they lost all their initial reservation and told me all I wanted to know. "Who is buried here?" I asked. "My sister-in-law," answered a dark young man. "She died five months ago in childbirth." Then he introduced me to his widowed brother and three little children, who were sitting quietly around the grave. The other members of the family just looked on. After some more exchanges, I knelt down on the graveside, said some silent prayers, and blessed the living and the dead. When I rose, the two brothers asked me with some anxiety: "What did you pray?" I said: "I prayed that the Lord will lead your wife and sister-in-law into his home, that he will give new strength and courage to all the members of your family, and that he will bring peace to your country." Everyone expressed a sense of relief and gratitude. "Thank you very much, thank you, thank you," they said as they shook my hand with affection.

When I left the cemetery, many thoughts ran through my mind. What had I witnessed? What did all of this mean? Most central to all the impressions I had received was the impression that I had seen something very deep, old, basic, and human. The gatherings around the graves, the food on the blankets, the human-shaped breads, the praying boys, the exchange of gifts, and the all-pervading spirit of gentleness and hospitality: all of that seemed to come from ages past, even from far beyond the time when the Gospel of Jesus was first brought to Latin America. Most of the inhabitants of Cochabamba are Quechua Indians, and their Christianity is pervaded with the religious convictions and practices of the Quechua culture. Although Our Fathers and Hail Marys are constantly recited, it seemed that they only partially express the power of Indian spirituality.

I felt very much part of a mystery that cannot simply be observed and understood, and I started to sympathize even more with the sisters and priests who, after many years in Bolivia, say: "We still can only partially grasp the depth of the Quechua soul." One image stayed uppermost in my mind. It was the image of the boys receiving food for their prayers. The food put on the graves to be eaten with the dead was given to those who prayed for them. In front of my eyes I saw how prayers became food and food became prayers. I saw how little boys who had to struggle to survive received life from the dead, and how the dead received hope from the little children who prayed for the salvation of their souls. I saw a profound communion between the living and the dead, an intimacy expressed in words and gestures whose significance easily escapes our practical and often skeptical minds. The little children, as well as some of the older blind and crippled people, were allowed to enter into communication with the dead, while the adults remained silent, watched, and handed out gifts. "Out of the mouths of babes" we hear the truth, and by them the mysteries of life are revealed to us.

When I returned home, I knew that the Indians had given me a glimpse of a reality that mostly remains hidden in my rational, well-planned, and well-protected life. I had heard voices, seen faces, and touched hands revealing a divine love in which the living and the dead can find a safe home. In the evening I celebrated the Eucharist with friends in the language school. It seemed to me that all who had been part of this day—my family members and friends for whom I had prayed in the early morning, the medical doctor, the students and teachers, the Indian people of Cochabamba and their dead, as well as all the people who live and die on this earth—were gathered around the table. When the bread and the cup, the body and blood of Our Lord, were shared, I felt even more a part of the mysterious interchange I had witnessed in the cemetery. Yes, we all are one people loved by One Lord who became food and drink for us all and thus took away whatever may separate the living from the dead.

Tonight I saw the movie *All Quiet on the Western Front,* which shows how the members of a German platoon are physically and mentally destroyed in the trenches of the First World War. It brought home the insanity of young German men killing young French men without knowing why.

Meanwhile, the world powers are preparing for a war so massive and devastating that there won't be many left to tell the story or make a movie of it. Samuel Cohen, the father of the neutron bomb, does not believe that a third world war can be avoided. In an interview published on the first of November in *Los Tiempos,* the Catholic daily newspaper printed in La Paz, Cohen expresses his pride in having invented this instrument that "kills but does not destroy." He says, "I never think 'my God, what did I invent?' I am conscious that this bomb is the most selective weapon ever invented. A weapon such as this never existed." In response to the question: "Do you believe that we will have another war?" he says: "Yes . . . I consider this simply to be part of human nature: struggle, death and war . . . and in all wars both parties will take in hand all the possible arms. . . . Nuclear weapons will be used in their total potential."

Reading this after having seen *All Quiet on the Western Front,* I try to imagine the horrible quiet that will hover over our planet if Cohen's prediction comes true. Will there be anyone to mourn the dead or to consider the rebuilding of a human community? The only words that can offer comfort are the words Jesus spoke: "Stay awake, praying at all times for the strength to survive all that is going to happen, and to stand with confidence before the Son of Man" (Luke 21:36). O Lord, have mercy on us.

Tonight Ed Moore, a Maryknoll priest who was involved in leadership training in Guatemala, and Tom Henehan, a Maryknoller who is doing similar work in Santiago, Chile, shared their ideas and experiences with the students of the language school. One thing was clear to me: those who are trained in leadership roles quickly become targets of the oppressors. When politicians realize that the Indians are no longer passive, dependent beings who can be exploited, but have become a people educated to speak with a clear voice, they respond with oppression, torture, and murder. I was struck with the fact that often education means preparation for martyrdom. This is no argument for not educating. Those who have become aware of the nature of their captivity and have seen what is necessary to change the system never regret what they have learned, even though their knowledge may cost them their lives.

One of Ed's observations helped me see how quickly politics enters the picture. Many young people who have been trained as evangelizers, health promotors, or social-change agents soon become aware of the political nature of the physical, mental, and spiritual poverty of their people. This awareness frequently leads them to enter directly into the political arena; they strive to become mayor of their town or to acquire other political offices.

Another observation made by Tom explained why foreign missioners are so frequently accused of political involvement. In general, they are the ones who work most closely with the poor, the homeless, and the jobless, because they are the only ones who can afford to do so. The local pastoral workers need to earn money to survive, not only for themselves but also for parents and siblings who look to them for support. Thus they are forced to accept income-producing jobs such as teaching in grade school, high school, or university. Foreign missioners, on the other hand, are supported by their congregations at home, and thus have the freedom to live and work with the poor. Thus it is quite understandable that many oppressive governments make the foreign priests, sisters, and lay missioners the target of their hostility and condemn them as communist subversives.

Meanwhile, I try to remember that Jesus was killed as a subversive. God, who became human, submitted himself to the manipulation and oppression of the political powers of his time. He died under the accusation of being the enemy of the ruling class. It was not without reason that Pilate placed above Jesus' head the charge: "This is Jesus, the King of the Jews." Can we be true Christians without being considered to be subversives in the eyes of the oppressors?

I am reading a fascinating chapter from Jerry Mander's book *Four Arguments for the Elimination of Television.* The main idea is: "We evolve into the images we carry in our minds. We become what we see. And in today's America, what most of us see is one hell of a lot of television."

I had heard stories about Vietnam veterans who, during their first real battle, thought that it was just another war movie and were shocked when those they killed did not stand up and walk away. I had read that Vincent van Gogh saw the real world as an imitation of the paintings he saw in the museum. I had noticed how children often are more excited about the repeated advertisements on television than about the movie they interrupt. But I had never fully thought through the enormous impact of the artificially imposed images on my thoughts, feelings, and actions. When it is true that the image you carry in your mind can affect your physical, mental, and emotional life, then it becomes a crucial question as to which images we expose ourselves or allow ourselves to be exposed.

All of this is important to me because it has profound spiritual implications. Prayer also has much to do with imagining. When I bring myself into the presence of God, I imagine him in many ways: as a loving father, a supporting sister, a caring mother, a severe teacher, an honest judge, a fellow traveler, an intimate friend, a gentle healer, a challenging leader, a demanding taskmaster. All these "personalities" create images in my mind that affect not only what I think, but also how I actually experience myself. I believe that true prayer makes us into what we imagine. To pray to God leads to becoming like God.

When Saint Ignatius proposes that we use all our senses in our meditation, he does more than offer a technique to help us concentrate on the mysteries of God's revelation. He wants us to imagine the reality of the divine as fully as possible so that we can slowly be divinized by that reality. Divinization is, indeed, the goal of all prayer and meditation. This divinization allows St. Paul to say: "I live now not with my own life but with the life of Christ who lives in me" (Gal. 2:20).

The more we come to depend on the images offered to us by those who try to distract us, entertain us, use us for their purposes, and make us conform to the demands of a consumer society, the easier it is for us to lose our identity. These imposed images actually make us into the world which they represent, a world of hatred, violence, lust, greed, manipulation, and oppression. But when we believe that we are created in the image of God himself and come to realize that Christ came to let us reimagine this, then meditation and prayer can lead us to our true identity.

These considerations reveal the intimate bond between ministry and the life of prayer and meditation. Because what else is ministry than witnessing to him whom "we have heard, and we have seen with our own eyes; . . . watched and touched with our hands" (1 John 1:1)? Ministry is the manifestation in our own person of the presence of Christ in the world. The more fully we have imagined who we truly are and the more our true identity becomes visible, the more we become living witnesses of Jesus Christ. This means much more than speaking and acting in the Name of Him who came to us long ago. It means that our words and actions themselves become a manifestation of the living Christ here and now.

Latin America offers us the image of the suffering Christ. The poor we see every day, the stories about deportation, torture, and murder we hear every day, and the undernourished children we touch every day, reveal to us the suffering Christ hidden within us. When we allow this image of the suffering Christ within us to grow into its full maturity, then ministry to the poor and oppressed becomes a real possibility; because then we can indeed hear, see, and touch him within us as well as among us. Thus prayer becomes ministry and ministry becomes prayer. Once we have seen the suffering Christ within us, we will see him wherever we see people in pain. Once we have seen the suffering Christ among us, we will recognize him in our innermost self. Thus we come to experience that the first commandment to love God with all your heart, with all your soul and with all your mind, resembles indeed the second: "You must love your neighbor as yourself" (Matt. 22:39–40).

Friday, November 6

Tonight the students and staff of the language school celebrated a special Eucharist of solidarity with the Church in the prelature of Juli in Peru. Bill McCarthy, the Maryknoller who came from

Lima to attend a conference here, was the main celebrant; and Sister Lourdes, who works in Juli and is currently studying Aymara (the language of the Aymara Indians, who live in the Altiplano), gave the homily and sang a Spanish song, which she composed herself. A small sculpture of an Indian carrying a heavy load on his back, a plate with incense, flowers, and a candle were placed in the center of the circle to symbolize the suffering, the prayers, and the hope of the poor in Juli. There also was a broken glass and a stone to remind us of the violence that has occurred there recently.

The main reason for this celebration was to call attention to the day of prayer that will take place in Juli on November fifteenth. On that day, Christians from all over Peru will come to Juli to make a prayerful response to the first signs of persecution of the Church in Peru. Sister Lourdes herself was present at the Institute for Rural Education when it was attacked by forty masked men.

As I listened to Bill's explanation of the symbols and to Lourdes' words about fear, hope, and the importance of being faithful, I could not prevent myself from thinking that all of this might be the beginning of a confrontation that can take on dimensions much greater than we now can imagine. What will result from the demonstration on November fifteenth? There are many people who hate the Church because of its support for the poor. Will they see the day of prayer as a reason to intensify the oppression or as a challenge to conversion? It is hard to say. Protest is required by our faithfulness to the poor. But nobody knows if things will become better or worse. I fear the worst, but hope that November fifteenth will make it clear that the Church won't back off from its promises to support the poor at all times.

The songs were joyful, the readings hopeful, and the sharing of the Body and Blood of Our Lord a true expression of community. The celebration allowed us to remind ourselves that we are already part of the kingdom even though we are still living in the valley of tears. It is becoming clearer to me every day that one of the greatest gifts offered to Christians is the possibility of celebrating not only their newly found freedom, but also the captivity to which they are still subjected. In the Christian community, joy and sorrow are never separated. Our joy witnesses to the awareness that nothing can separate us from the Lord of life, our sorrow reminds us that the way of the Lord of life is the way of the cross.

Saturday, November 7

Today was a day filled with letter writing. I wrote to my brother and his wife to express to them my support and love as they struggle to offer a safe and loving home to their little daughter Laura. I wrote to my aunt and uncle to offer them a word of comfort as they grieve for the death of their daughter Rosemarie, who died a few years after they lost their daughter Magdaleen. I wrote to my priest friend, Henny, who lost both of his parents within a few weeks. I wrote to my cousin who lost her husband shortly before she gave birth to her second child.

I now feel tired and emotionally drained. As I let all these pains in the lives of my family and friends enter into my heart, I wondered how I could offer true comfort. How could I ever enter into their pain and offer hope from that place? How could I enter into real solidarity with them? But then I slowly realized that I do not have to be like them or to carry their burdens, but that our Lord, my Lord and their Lord, has carried all human burdens and was crushed by them, so that we could receive his Spirit, the comforter. I realize now that my first task is to pray that this comforting Spirit will reach the hearts and minds of all those to whom I have written today. I hope that my halting and stuttering letters will be received as an expression of my sincere prayer that what is beyond my ability to touch can be touched by the consoling and healing power of the God whose name is Love.

Monday, November 9

Today I found new living quarters. During the weekend I had become aware that I was speaking too much English and that I needed a total immersion in the Spanish language.

The Quiroga family, who live about a half-hour walk from the institute, offered me their generous hospitality. It is a joy to be here. Mr. and Mrs. Quiroga are very kind and quite willing to correct my Spanish, and their twelve-year-old son, Rodolfito, is excited to have someone in the house with whom he can practice his English.

Rodolfo Senior and his wife, Nancy, lived for eight years in Miami. During that time they learned some English, although the predominantly Cuban population did not encourage them to practice it. But because their son went to school there, he became much more fluent in English than his parents. When the family returned to Bolivia more than four years ago, Rodolfito continued in an English-speaking grade school. Although he now goes to the Spanish-speaking Catholic high school in Cochabamba, he continues to practice his English on the American guests who come to his home. Rodolfo is a businessman in Cochabamba, and Nancy is an enthusiastic shortwave radio amateur, who speaks daily with people from all over the world: Indonesia, Thailand, Poland, Holland, the States, and many other countries.

One of the best parts of living with the Quiroga family is that they all like to talk. I am always surrounded by Spanish sounds, and I hope that these sounds will become more and more familiar to me.

Tuesday, November 10

Last night Rodolfo Quiroga told me the story of his life. He was born in Oruro, the city of the tin mines. His parents were simple, hardworking people. Five of their nine children died during their first months. "Poor climate and poor medical help," Rodolfo explained.

When Rodolfo was eight years old, the son of the owner of the house in which they lived, a seventeen-year-old boy known for his morbid desire to hurt animals, walked into the house with a pistol and killed Rodolfo's ten-year-old brother. Rodolfo's parents were out of their minds with grief. For many days his father woke up during the night, walked around the house with a gun, and spoke wildly about revenge. But when he realized that he still had a caring wife and three boys who needed him, he slowly became a different man. While he had always been a fervent atheist and was married under the condition that the Church would have nothing to do with him and his family, he suddenly turned to God in his grief and became a man who committed his life to prayer, charity, and the spiritual well-being of his family. Both he and his wife started to go to church every day. Soon afterwards, their three sons were baptized and received their first communion. The house of this simple family became a place of faith and hope.

Alex, one of the sons, studied philosophy with the Jesuits for some years and contemplated joining their Society; but he had to leave because of poor health. Alex is currently a professor of Spanish literature in Massachusetts, a very active Christian who introduced the Marriage Encounter movement in Cochabamba. Max, the second son, is an accountant, who after many years in La Paz moved to Cochabamba to give his sickly wife a better climate in which to live. Rodolfo, my host, joined the religious congregation of the Servites for a few years, but had to leave them to support his family when his mother became ill. He married Nancy soon after his return home. Their first two children died. A few years after Rodolfito was born, they adopted a boy who died unexpectedly in his third month of life. Now their twelve-year-old son Rodolfito is the center of their life.

I was moved by this story and the simple and loving way in which Rodolfo told it. For him it was God's story as much as his own. It was a story about suffering, but a suffering in which God had become present and shown his love. When Rodolfo told me his life, he seemed to be speaking more about God's love than about his own struggles. His voice was full of gratitude and praise. No anger, no resentment, no feelings of revenge. He spoke with the quick knowledge that God has guided his life and will continue to do so, no matter what happens.

Wednesday, November 11

Last night Rodolfo celebrated his fifty-second birthday. To me it seemed like an old-fashioned Dutch birthday party. Family and friends kept coming during the evening to congratulate Rodolfo and his wife. As it got later, the circle became larger, the conversation more animated and the voices louder. Everyone was happy and everyone was everyone else's entertainment. No television, radio, music, or slides; just good lively exchanges of home news, town news, and family news, real or made up for the occasion. The food and wine led to the traditional birthday cake which was—to my surprise—welcomed with the American song "Happy Birthday to You."

The evening was of special interest to me because I had a long conversation with Peter, the recently ordained Polish priest who is studying with me at language school and had become a friend of the Quiroga family. Peter's story moved me and awoke in me emotions that had remained hidden for a long time.

During all of his life, Peter had lived in Poland. As a teenager he was not very religious, but he was a good youth leader. A Dominican priest evoked in him the desire for the priesthood. First he thought about becoming a Dominican; but a short time before entering the Dominican novitiate, he met a priest of the Divine Word Society who spoke to him about their missions. Peter felt that this was a providential encounter and he decided to join the Divine Word Society in the hope that one day he could be a missionary in Japan, Korea, or Taiwan. Six months ago, Peter was ordained. But instead of being sent to any of the countries he hoped for, his superiors sent him to Bolivia to learn Spanish in preparation for three years of mission work in Paraguay.

Peter impressed me deeply from the moment I first saw him among the other students of the language school. He has a fine, youthful face that makes him look like a very tender boy; he does not speak one word of English, but his Spanish is remarkable for the short time he has been studying it. Although there is one other Polish priest and two Polish sisters in the institute, he avoids them; he is determined not to utter one Polish word before Christmas. As a result, he learns Spanish faster than anyone else I know.

The first thing Peter expressed to me was a deep sadness that mothers in Poland no longer have the necessary food for their newborn babies. There is such a lack of milk, butter, and other crucial nutrients that the number of abortions in Catholic Poland is staggering. "It is terrible," Peter kept saying. "It is the great sin of our nation. In the few months since I have been a priest, I have heard the confession of so many men and women who agonize over their inability to care for children. But abortion is no solution."

And slowly Peter revealed to me his deep faith, which is intimately connected with his love for his people. "We in Poland desire only two types of freedom: freedom from sin and freedom from foreign domination. Every father and every mother speaks to their children about these freedoms, which are more important for us than food, a house, or material success." With strong emotion, Peter spoke about the faith of his people. "Being Polish and being Catholic is the same for us. We are not interested in politics, in war, in power. We have never started a war. What we desire is to live a life close to God and the Virgin Mother. There is no house in Poland without a picture of Our Lady of Czestochowa, and, I tell you, miracles happen every day to those who bring their sufferings to her. And the Communists? They have the power, they give away the key positions, they make all the decisions, they rule the country. But the heart of the thirty million Poles is not with them. The people pray, the people go to Mass, the people come together in their houses for religious instruction, and that is where you come to understand the Polish soul."

When Peter spoke about John Paul II, I could sense strong feelings surge up in him. John Paul was given to his people to offer them new courage and a new hope for freedom. I came to see in Peter's eyes that John Paul was indeed the mysterious answer of God to decades of fervent Polish prayers. Since John Paul had become Pope, hundreds of young people had entered seminaries and religious life. Now there are thirty major seminaries and each has at least one hundred students. Talking about John Paul, Peter said: "When he was shot, most people in the world were reading the papers or watching television to follow the events, but the Poles all went to their churches and prayed." Moreover, Peter was convinced that without John Paul there would probably have been no Solidarity movement. Peter said: "The Poles listened to every word John Paul said during his visit to Poland. He always spoke about the Spirit of God that all of us have received and that is the basis of our true freedom. His words gave us strength, self-confidence, and the courage to claim our own rights. I think indeed that John Paul had a lot to do with the origin of Solidarity, not directly, but certainly indirectly."

There was not a trace of triumphalism in Peter's voice. It was clear that he spoke as a man who had suffered oppression, exploitation, and hunger although I felt that at times he overlooked some important questions (such as the suffering of Polish Jews in the past and the present), he radiated a simple solid faith that allowed him to speak about God, Jesus, Mary, the Church, and the Pope with an intimacy and familiarity that made me jealous.

He told me about his departure. His father and mother told him: "You are a priest now; be sure to pray always, wherever you are; never let a day go by without saying the rosary." Peter had tears in his eyes when he told me this. "If I just had a little bit of my parents' faith! They are such simple, poor, and faithful people. They truly know what counts. They do not want me to be important, powerful, successful. The only thing they hope is that I will be a man of prayer who leads others closer to God. They know nothing about Bolivia or Paraguay, but they pray for me and for all the people I am sent to."

Peter opened deep places in me. His whole being radiated commitment to God and to his Church, and I sensed that I was in the presence of a man of faith, a faith that I had not seen for a long time. And somewhere, too, Peter gave me a new glimpse of that remarkable—and often disturbing—holy man, John Paul II.

Thursday, November 12

It suddenly hit me. The United States wants war! It is frightening to write this sentence down, but during the last week the thought that the Reagan Administration is not only preparing for the possibility of a war, but is even directly moving towards it, kept haunting me. For a few days, the idea of an approaching war in which a destruction of life and culture would take place such as history has never witnessed kept me restless during the day and sleepless during the night. Looking at the movements of the U.S. government from the perspective of this utterly poor, helpless, and dependent country is a quite different experience than looking at it from within the United States. Living in the United States allows you to maintain the illusion that the arms race, the joint military exercises in Egypt, the sale of the AWACS planes to Saudi Arabia, and especially the Cancun conference in Mexico, are all movements to keep the peace. But living here in Bolivia, surrounded by increasing poverty and human misery, the face of the United States becomes uglier and uglier as the days progress.

What frightens me most is the shift in the popular expectation of war. Although there is no Hitler raving about the superiority of the Aryan race, although there is no visible advantage to any country to become involved in an international conflict, the majority of the American people expect a world war in the near future and few believe that an all-out nuclear holocaust can be avoided.

During the last few weeks, most of the U.S. weeklies as well as the major foreign publications have filled their pages with speculations about an impending war. What most frightens me is the predominantly military responses of the U.S. government to the main problems in the world. *Newsweek* (November 9, 1981) writes: "Reagan had relied mainly on a display of military might: his

White House has struck arms deals with El Salvador, Venezuela, and Pakistan, promised to speed up arms shipments to Egypt and the Sudan and invited China to shop at America's weapons bazaar." Behind this show of power is the desire to give the American people the sense of being in control. One of Reagan's top advisers says: "The bottom line is that America is tired of being shoved around and [Reagan has] taken care of that." But the more I think about the lack of genuine diplomacy between Moscow and Washington, the growing tensions in Poland, the extremely fragile situation in the Middle East, the increasing U.S. support to South Africa, and the blatant U.S. help to the "authoritarian" right-wing military regimes in the Southern hemisphere to counteract the so-called totalitarian influence of Cuba in Central America—all of this in the context of the biggest "peacetime" military buildup in the history of the United States—the more I wonder whether there is any serious attempt to ensure peace. I fear that the increasing economic problems not only of the third world countries but also of the United States and Europe may become the occasion to try out some of the apocalyptic toys on which the Pentagon relies so much. Even after Vietnam, we seem to believe that weapons can make peace. They can certainly make war, but today a war no longer can have peace at the other end, only total annihilation.

Meanwhile, words remain extremely dangerous. We now hear words about a nuclear warning attack, words about occupying Cuba or invading Nicaragua. Such words by people in power, with their subsequent denials, create an ongoing atmosphere of anxiety and may eventually lead to mistakes, the consequences of which cannot be overestimated.

It is in the context of this international situation that Christians have to make their choice for peace. Personally, I sometimes feel so engulfed by the political realities that I wonder if a world conflict can be avoided. The main question for me is: Do I "have the strength to survive all that is going to happen, and to stand with confidence before the Son of Man" (Luke 21:36)? Or will I allow myself and others to be so overwhelmed by all these wars and rumors of war that we will die of fear as we await what menaces the world? Am I really ready to encounter my Lord when he comes in a "cloud with power and great glory" (Luke 21: 26–27)?

How much time and energy we spend in understanding, analyzing, discussing, and evaluating the socioeconomic and political status of our globe, and how little of our hearts and minds is occupied to prepare ourselves for the day of the Lord, which will be sprung on us suddenly, "like a trap" (Luke 21:35). Prayer, meditation, fasting, communal life, care for the sick, the dying, the hungry, and the fearful, are they really in the center of our lives as Christian people? The world is coming to an end, probably by our own doing, and this will happen this week, this decade, this century, or millions of years in the future; but the certainty of an end should give us the strength to announce boldly and fearlessly that those who hold on to the Lord of life will not be harmed but have eternal life. But woe to us when, on the day of the Lord, "hearts will be coarsened with debauchery and drunkenness and the cares of life" (Luke 21:34).

All of this suggests to me the urgent need for a spirituality that takes the end of things very seriously, not a spirituality of withdrawal, nor of blindness to the powers of the world, but a spirituality that allows us to live in this world without belonging to it, a spirituality that allows us to taste the joy and peace of the divine life even when we are surrounded by the powers and principalities of evil, death, and destruction. I wonder if a spirituality of liberation does not need to be deepened by a spirituality of exile or captivity. I wonder if a spirituality that focuses on the alleviation of poverty should not be deepened by a spirituality that allows people to continue their lives when their poverty only increases. I wonder if a spirituality that encourages peacemaking should not be deepened by a spirituality that allows us to remain faithful when the only things we see are dying children, burning houses, and the total destruction of our civilization. May God prevent any of these horrors from taking place, may we do all that is possible to prevent them, but may we never lose our faith when "great misery [descends] on the land and wrath on this people, . . . [when there are] signs in the sun and moon and stars, . . . [when] nations [are] in agony, bewildered by the clamor of the ocean and its waves" (Luke 21:24–26). I pray that we will not be swept away by our own curiosity, sensationalism, and panic, but remain attentive to Him who comes and will say: "Come, you whom my Father has blessed, take for your heritage the kingdom prepared for you since the foundation of the world" (Matt. 25:34–35).

One of the best articles I have read about the plight of the Latin American Church was published in Lent 1981 in the *National Catholic Reporter*. It is written by an anonymous American priest working in Bolivia. The author preferred to remain anonymous in order to prevent reprisals against himself and those with whom he works. From the depth of his heart he cries out to his fellow Christians in the United States, begging them to listen, to understand and to act. He writes:

> What we see is this. The documents of the Latin American bishops' meetings at both Medellin and Puebla . . . condemn "liberal capitalism" by name along with atheistic communism and ideologies of national security. Neither the U.S. Catholic bishops nor priests, with rare exceptions, teach the implications of this doctrine in the ethical formation of U.S. Catholics. We think this is a grave dereliction of duty which has terrible human consequences.
>
> We see these consequences every day. Assassination, physical and psychological torture and rape are the ordinary judicial means of inquiry in our countries. These intelligence skills have been taught for 35 years to more than 80,000 Latin American military and police forces as counter-insurgent and anti-terrorist tactics to keep the "Communists" from invading our economic sphere of influence. You would want proof? Get names and addresses from the bishops of Chile, Brazil, Argentina, Bolivia, El Salvador, etc., as well as from Amnesty International.
>
> Latin Americans do not want to be satellites of the superpowers, neither of Russia nor the United States. They want to be free of economic and political colonialism. And they are not permitted to be. By force and physical violence, every normal avenue of social and political change is closed to them. Or must we accept the opinion that violence is the only "normal" path to a healthy human society? . . .
>
> For the first time in their tortured history, Salvadoreans, Guatemalans, Peruvians, Brazilians, etc., want the right to be themselves. They want the right to make their own mistakes in their own path to maturity as a people with identity and responsibility. No one can stop this march of history. . . .
>
> Latin America in the year 2000 will have 500 million people, half of them under 21 with creative energy and youthful aspirations. The United States, with its own anti-life culture which considers children as the enemy of conspicuous consumption, will be a nation of old people and old ideas, spent, sterile, wasted and without a future. . . .

The coming generations of young Latin Americans will hate the
people of the United States if we continue our greedy ways. How
long can we keep these hordes controlled to provide us with our
more than comfortable lifestyle if they learn how to read and write?

After these words, this anonymous author addresses himself to
parishioners, bishops, and priests, theologians and intellectuals,
men and women religious, union members and workers, and
finally to the young:

Do not sell your faith or your freedom to maintain the antique shop
called "western civilization." Whatever it may have been in the
18th and 19th centuries, it has not been for the 20th. And it offers
no hope to youth for their century, the 21st. . . . The political and
economic systems, theories and practices we have seen for 35 years
offer nothing but a musty nostalgia. The smell of death is upon
them. . . .

We, your mission representatives, do not ask you to wallow in
unproductive guilt. We ask you to change your priorities. And the
priorities of our nation. You will then be free. And so will millions
of others whose slavery and poverty are now the basis of your good
life. How can people of conscience and faith be at peace with
themselves or their society knowing what their comfort costs others?

And he concludes with these powerful words:

As for ourselves, we know that we now have, no security and no
protection from either our host countries or the colonial power of
the United States government always acting behind the scenes. We
have no arms except the armor of faith and the shield of hope. We
are free as never before to give witness to the life of Jesus as did
the sisters in El Salvador. "We are cursed and we bless. . . ." We
are condemned as "subversives," "agitators," "Communists," "foreigners" wherever we unmask the idolatry of money and power.
We are imprisoned, tortured, expelled, or killed for living the gospel. . . . Our mission task now is to tell the Americans to convert,
to "let my people go," to seek a just and fraternal human life with
the poor of Latin America and the world. Or to see the United States
destroy itself, its youth and its future, by stupid, selfish, useless,
endless greed and violence. There is no liberation, no resurrection
without conversion and the death of old ways ("A Cry for Latin
America," *National Catholic Reporter,* April 17, 1981).

Living here in Bolivia, seeing the tired faces of the women who
carry their heavy burdens to the market, seeing the undernourished children, seeing miserable fruit vendors and beggars and

realizing that things are getting worse and worse day after day, I know that this cry from and for Latin America doesn't hold any sentimentality, sensationalism, or false rhetoric.

Saturday, November 14

As the days and weeks pass by and I come to know the students of the language school better, I realize more and more how insecure, fearful, and often lonely many of us are. Not only do we continue to hope for mail from "home," but we also continue to be submerged by the powers around us. At home we at least had our own niche in life, our own little place where we could feel useful and admired. Here none of that is present. Here we are in a world that did not invite us, in which we can hardly express ourselves and which constantly reminds us of our powerlessness. And still, we know that we are sent here, that God wants us here, and that it is here that we have to work out our salvation.

The more these strong and often conflicting feelings come to the surface, the more I realize how much we need each other. Mission work is not a task for individuals. The Lord sent his disciples into the world in small groups, not as individual heroes or pioneers. We are sent out together, so that together—gathered by One Lord—we can make him present in this world.

Many of us are eager to go out and to start working as soon as possible, with or without words! It is certainly a sign of zeal, good will, great energy, and generosity. But maybe we should first of all look at each other, recognize each other's suffering and come together as a living body to pray, and to share our joys and hopes, our fears and pains. This experience of belonging to each other by our common love for Our Lord and our common awareness of our task can create the space where God's Spirit will descend and from where we can go out in many directions without ever feeling alone. After all, the first and most important witness is to them who can say of us: "See how they love each other."

Tuesday, November 17

I spent the afternoon with the children of the Catholic orphanage called Gotas de Leche (Drops of Milk). The children were so starved for affection that they fought with each other for the privilege of touching me.

How little do we really know the power of physical touch. These boys and girls only wanted one thing: to be touched, hugged, stroked, and caressed. Probably most adults have the same needs but no longer have the innocence and unself-consciousness to express them. Sometimes I see humanity as a sea of people starving for affection, tenderness, care, love, acceptance, forgiveness, and gentleness. Everyone seems to cry: "Please love me." The cry becomes louder and the response so inaudible that people kill each other and themselves in despair. The little orphans tell more than they know. If we don't love one another, we kill one another. There's no middle road.

Wednesday, November 18

My move to the Quiroga family hasn't made my prayer life easier. I spend much time going back and forth to the language institute, have a hard time keeping up with my four classes every day, and feel more tired than usual. The last two weeks I was not able to spend much time in prayer and had to limit myself to my breviary and the Eucharist. Life without prayer weakens my spirit. I have to start looking for a new rhythm. At least I know the difference between days with ample time for prayer and days that are hurried and restless.

Nobody has to prove to me that prayer makes a difference. Without prayer I become irritable, tired, heavy of heart, and I lose the Spirit who directs my attention to the needs of others instead of my own. Without prayer, my attention moves to my own preoccupation. I become cranky and spiteful and often I experience resentment and a desire for revenge.

I am surprised that I allow the language training to become so important that my prayer life takes a second place to it. It seems that when there are no urgent things to do, I create them myself, and when there are no deadlines to meet, I organize them for myself. That is a clear form of self-deception. The powers that try to keep me from simply being with God have a seductive quality. Something as simple as a language course can play demon with me. Why speak different languages if my heart remains dry and angry, upset and lonely? Everything is so obvious. To reach the obvious, I have to struggle. It is the struggle that Our Lord himself came to share.

In times of testing, God and the demon seem close together. Today I felt this more strongly than on other days. After classes I went to downtown Cochabamba to pick up Rodolfo's bicycle, which he was willing to lend me. As I biked through town and saw groups of young men loitering around the street corners and waiting for the next movie to start; as I walked through the bookstores stacked with magazines about violence, sex, and gossip; and as I saw the endless advertisements for unnecessary items imported mostly from Germany and the United States, I had the feeling of being surrounded by powers much greater than myself. I felt the seductive powers of sin all around me and got a glimpse of the truth that all the horrendous evils which plague our world—hunger, the nuclear arms race, torture, exploitation, rape, child abuse, and all forms of oppression—have their small and sometimes unnoticed beginnings in the human heart. The demon is very patient in the way he goes about his destructive work. I felt the darkness of the world all around me.

After some aimless wandering, I biked to the small Carmelite convent on Avenida America, close to the house of my hosts. A friendly Carmelite sister spoke to me in the chapel and told me that I would be welcome at any hour to come there to pray or celebrate the Eucharist. She radiated a spirit of joy and peace. She told me about the light that shines into the darkness without saying a word about it. As I looked around, I saw the statues of St. Teresa of Avila and St. Thérèse of Lisieux. Suddenly it seemed to me that these two women were talking to me as they had never before. They spoke of another world. As I knelt down in the small and simple chapel, I knew that this place was filled with God's presence. I felt the prayers that had been said there day and night.

After returning from the Carmelite sisters, I read the life of St. Thérèse of Lisieux in *Ten Christians,* a book that I had taken with me on my journey. Thérèse's unconditional love for Christ spoke to me in a new way. She dedicated her life to the missions and she considered herself a missionary in her hidden convent. She reminded me that true mission means being sent into the world as Christ was sent into the world: in total surrender to God's will.

My visit to the Carmelite sisters helped me realize again that where the demon is, God is not far away; and where God shows his presence, the demon does not remain absent very long. There is always a choice to be made between the power of life and the power of death. I myself have to make that choice. Nobody else, not even God, will make that choice for me.

This morning at 8:30 Gerry McCrane and Sister Lourdes gave a report to the students at the language school about their journey to Peru. They participated in the day of prayer in Juli on November fifteenth organized in response to the recent attacks on the local church. It was a moving report. Gerry and Lourdes told how five thousand poor *campesinos* walked from the house where the first attack took place to the cathedral. They showed how the Church of Juli had truly become the Church of the people. The people had grown aware over the years that the Church had become something other than a wealthy institution that tries to maintain the status quo. This transition was not as obvious as it might seem. Many of the organizers of the day of prayer had wondered what the response would be. Would people come and join in the pilgrimage? Would there be violence from those who had already shown their hostility by destruction and death threats? Would people get hurt in the crowds? What would be the response of those bishops who like to keep things quiet and who consider such actions provocative? These and many other questions had occupied the mind of Alberto Koenigsknecht, the prelate of Juli, and of his collaborators. The issue had been: "Are we doing more harm than good by calling the people of Peru to a public manifestation of their religious commitment in the face of a beginning persecution?"

But Sunday, November fifteenth, had been a day of solidarity for the poor, a day of sincere prayer, a day of mutual encouragement, and a day of recommitment to the work in Juli. Gerry, who had been pastor in Juli for many years, showed great joy as he gave his report: "It was such a source of gratitude to see that, after many years of hard pastoral work, the people had come to see and believe that they themselves are the Church and that they were willing to offer up a day good for planting to show it." And Lourdes told with excitement how hundreds of *campesinos* had worked together to prepare this day. Small pamphlets about the meaning of this special pilgrimage had been studied in the different parishes during the weeks preceding the day of prayer, and many hours had been spent to make this day not so much a protest against hostile behavior as a witness for Christ living in the people of the Juli prelature. The Eucharist, celebrated on the square in front of the cathedral, had been a true Aymara feast. Many Aymara symbols had been integrated into the celebration; this was not a Latin ritual imposed on poor Indians, but a true manifestation of the spirituality of the Aymara people.

I was glad to hear this story of faith and hope. For awhile I had thought about going with Gerry and Lourdes myself, but felt that language training had to remain my priority for the short time I am in Bolivia. Meanwhile, I wonder with some apprehension if this is the last word we will hear about the prelature of Juli. Where God's love becomes very visible, the forces of evil usually do not long remain hidden. Is the day in Juli the end of a short experience of persecution or the beginning of a long road of suffering on which the faith of many will be tested? I pray that all who work there and will work there will have the strength and the courage to be faithful.

Saturday, November 21

God exists. When I can say this with all that I am, I have the "gnosis" (the knowledge of God) about which St. John speaks and the "Memoria Dei" (the memory of God) about which St. Basil writes. To say with all that we have, think, feel, and are: "God exists," is the most world-shattering statement that a human being can make. When we make that statement, all the distinctions between intellectual, emotional, affective, and spiritual understanding fall away and there is only one truth left to acclaim: God exists. When we say this from the heart, everything trembles in heaven and on earth. Because when God exists, all that *is* flows from him. When I want to know if I ever have come to the true knowledge, the gnosis, of God's existence, I have simply to allow myself to become aware of how I experience myself. It doesn't take much to realize that I am constantly with myself. I am aware of all of the various parts of my body, and I "know" when I am hurting and when not. I am aware of my desire for food and clothing and shelter. I am aware of my sexual urges and my need for intimacy and community. I am aware of my feelings of pity, compassion, and solidarity, my ability to be of service and my hope to give a helping hand. I am aware of my intellectual, physical, and artistic skills and my drive to use them. I am aware of my anger, my lust, my feelings of revenge and resentment, and even at times of my desire to harm. Indeed, what is central to me is: *I exist.* My own existence fills me, and wherever I turn I find myself again locked in my own self-awareness: I exist. Although experiences of hatred are different from experiences of love, and although a desire for power is different from a desire to serve, they all are the same insofar as they identify *my* existence as what *really* counts.

However, as soon as I say, "God exists," my existence no longer can remain in the center, because the essence of the knowledge of God reveals my own existence as deriving its total being from his. That is the true conversion experience. I no longer let the knowledge of my existence be the center from which I derive, project, deduct, or intuit the existence of God; I suddenly or slowly find my own existence revealed to me in and through the knowledge of God. Then it becomes real for me that I can love myself and my neighbor only because God has loved me first. The life-converting experience is not the discovery that I have choices to make that determine the way I live out my existence, but the awareness that my existence itself is not in the center. Once I "know" God, that is, once I experience his love as the love in which all my human experiences are anchored, I can only desire one thing: to be in that love. "Being" anywhere else, then, is shown to be illusory and eventually lethal.

All of these reflections have taken a new urgency for me, during these weeks in Bolivia. It slowly dawned on me that so much, if not most, of our energy and attention goes to the question of our own existence. We wonder how we are doing, how we feel, how we will serve in Latin America, and how we will organize our next day, weekend, year, or decade. We try hard to make responsible and moral choices that give us a sense that at least we are searching in the right direction. But all of this, the good as well as the bad, the responsible as well as the irresponsible, the acts of lust as well as the acts of service, lose their power over us when we realize that God exists, before and after, in the past and in the future, now and forever, and that in and through the knowledge of that divine existence I might get a small glimpse of why there is an I and a he, she, we, and they. Then all questions have only one answer: God. What am I supposed to think about? About God, because all thoughts find their creative power in him. What am I supposed to say? His Word, because all my words are fruitful to the degree that they are a reflection of his. What am I supposed to do? His will, because his will is the loving desire that gave existence to all that is, myself included.

Is it better to be in Bolivia, in Peru, in the United States, or in Holland? Is it better to give a glass of water to a thirsty child or to work on a new world order in which children will no longer beg for water? Is it better to read a book or to walk on the street, to write a letter or bind the wounds of a dying man? Is it better to do this or that, say this or that, think about this or that? All these questions suddenly appear to me as false preoccupations, as a captivity in the illusory concern about my own existence, as an expression of my sick supposition that God depends on me, that his existence is derived from mine.

Nothing is real without deriving its reality from God. This was the great discovery of St. Francis when he suddenly saw the whole world in God's hands and wondered why God didn't drop it. St. Augustine, St. Teresa of Avila, St. John Vianney, and all the saints are saints precisely because for them the order of being was turned around and they saw, felt, and—above all—knew with their heart that outside God nothing is, nothing breathes, nothing moves, and nothing lives.

This makes me aware that the basis of all ministry rests not in the moral life but in the mystical life. The issue is not to live as well as we can, but to let our life be one that finds its source in the Divine Life.

God exists, and the meaning of all that I am depends totally on that knowledge. I wonder constantly if I am genuinely allowing my life to be determined by that truth. Maybe part of my reason for hesitating to embrace this truth fully is that it challenges me to give up all control over my life and to let God be God, my God, the God of my neighbor, and the God of all creation. But I also realize that as long as I do not "do" this, my life is an illusion and most of my energy is spoiled in trying to keep that illusion going.

Does all of this mean that my thoughts, plans, projects, and ideas no longer matter? That conclusion has been drawn by people who used the spiritual life as a way to manipulate others and that conclusion has led, sadly enough, to false views on asceticism, obedience, surrender to God's will, and certain forms of self-denial. The converted person does not say that nothing matters anymore, but that everything that is happens in God and that he is the dwelling place where we come to know the true order of things. Instead of saying: "Nothing matters any more, since I know that God exists," the converted person says: "All is now clothed in divine light and therefore nothing can be unimportant." The converted person sees, hears, and understands with a divine eye, a divine ear, a divine heart. The converted person knows himself or herself and all the world in God. The converted person *is* where God is, and from that place everything matters: giving water, clothing the naked, working for a new world order, saying a prayer, smiling at a child, reading a book, and sleeping in peace. All has become different while all remains the same.

Somehow I feel that all these reflections are important for me in a time during which I have to make some very concrete decisions. The "nothing matters" and the "everything matters" should never be separated in a time such as this. What brings them together is the unceasing cry coming from the heart: "God exists."

Sunday, November 22

This morning for two hours I played with the little boys and girls at the state orphanage. This orphanage is much worse than Drops of Milk, the Catholic orphanage. About a hundred little kids were running around in a poorly kept stony yard surrounded by a large fence. The kids jumped all over me trying to be touched, to attract attention, to play, and to be lifted up. What struck me most was their explicit interest in my body. They kept stroking my forehead, saying, "What a large forehead!" They wanted to see my teeth, my tongue, and kept comparing the size of their hands and fingers with mine. Their fascination with a large person moved me. One six-year-old looked at me and said, "A grown man!" For her I symbolized a world from which she is excluded. These children see mostly other children. They have very few adults around who can help them see beyond themselves. Very soon I was transformed into a climbing tree. The kids tried to climb over my knees, chest, and shoulders to the top, and at one point there was a line of ten little ones waiting for their turn to climb the big man.

I fell in love with a little deaf-mute boy who was able with his expressive hands and eyes to explain to me whatever he wanted me to do. Everytime I did something—connecting a cord to his toy, making a knot in his piece of rope, tying his shoes—he gave me a big smile and put his arms around me.

None of these children has a home. The food they receive is minimal, the attention meager, and the education poor. What will become of them? Who will give them what they need? In a poor country the children always suffer the most.

In the afternoon I celebrated the feast of Christ the King with the Carmelite sisters. The children were on my mind when I took the bread and wine and said: "This is my body, this is my blood." The Lord became flesh and blood for these children; so they could touch him, hug him, kiss him, stroke him. And thus he is their friend, their brother. Jesus died naked on the cross with the words above his head: "This is the King of the Jews." Many of the kids walked around naked, jumping in and out of a cement tub of water, and running up to me to be hugged and kissed and to let my hands touch their skin and squeeze their little bodies. The naked King on the Cross and the naked kids in Cochabamba belong together. The God who is love stands with the children who crave love. I knew that I had seen my King again. He seems to say: "Come back. I will be here every day, every week, every year. I stay here because I became body and blood for them. Come and touch me."

Monday, November 23

Rodolfo Quiroga could hardly be a less political man. He never attends any meetings other than those of the Christian Family Movement, and he spends all his free time with his wife and son. He enjoys taking care of his flowers, making little repairs in his house, and joining his wife in her ham radio hobby. He is one of the most homebound men I have ever met and his conversations focus on his family, his religion, and occasionally—and somewhat reluctantly—on his business.

And yet a little over a year ago, at two o'clock one morning, a group of armed men appeared at his door and asked for entrance. When Rodolfo refused to let them in, they broke open his front door, forced him into their car, and took him off to prison. Nancy, Rodolfito, and the maid, Marcelita, were left in fear and confusion.

Early the next day, with the influence of her friends, Nancy got access to the head of the police and was able to find out what had happened and where Rodolfo was. It turned out that a family member with whom they had a long-standing personal conflict had called the military authorities and told them that Rodolfo was a Communist and was using his house for a conspiracy with his leftist friends to overthrow the government. The reaction had been immediate. The paramilitary police—mostly Argentinians trained in sinister duties and hired by the Bolivian government—were called and sent off to arrest Rodolfo. With brute force, they entered his house and took him to an overcrowded prison cell.

When Nancy spoke to the head of the police, one of his first questions was, "Do you know anyone who might like to harm your husband?" When Nancy told him about the conflict with the family member, the officer recognized that this was the same story he had already heard from Rodolfo himself and he told her about the phone call and the accusations. Since the Quirogas have many influential friends in Cochabamba, excuses were quickly made and within two hours Rodolfo was set free. The police officer even offered Nancy breakfast, but nobody offered to pay for the damage to the house.

This story might be read as a comedy of errors, but it illustrates one of the most familiar aspects of Latin American politics, the intimate connection between political and family conflicts. I think it will be hard ever to understand the complex political situations in Latin America without realizing how often old and bitter family conflicts are intermingled with the uses of political power. Objectively, nobody could be less likely to be considered a Communist, a political agitator, a conspirator, or even a public figure than Rodolfo, but he came close to being tortured or killed because of his alleged involvement in a fictitious political event.

All of this reminded me of the story of Dr. Joel Filártiga, my Paraguayan friend, whose seventeen-year-old son was tortured to death in 1976 to silence his own political resistance. Dr. Filártiga is a longtime opponent of the dictatorship of General Alfredo Stroessner. He publicly—through writing and drawing—criticizes his government. But his son would never have been abducted and cruelly murdered if the police inspector Americo Peña, who supervised the torture of the boy with electric shocks, had not also had a long-standing conflict with the Filártiga family.

In small countries such as Paraguay and Bolivia, there are only a few candidates for political office, and these few frequently have as many personal conflicts between themselves as political differences. Often it is difficult to figure out who is against whom and for what reason. The word "Communist" always comes in as a handy word to get the guns out of the closet, but it might well be that an unpaid loan or an offensive word is the real reason for destroying someone's life.

Little Rodolfito now is terribly afraid to be alone in the house. He bites his nails and worries about going away from home without his parents. The sight of his father being dragged out of his home continues to haunt him. Meanwhile, Nancy and Rodolfo endure many sleepless nights wondering what the next move of their enemy will be. I have begun to see why they both spend so many hours during the weekend playing with their ham radio and talking to friendly people from other parts of the world: it is safe company and a good distraction.

Tuesday, November 24

Tonight Sister Maria Rieckelman spoke about the problems of acculturation. She gave a fine presentation about the many psychological struggles we can experience when we try to find a home in a new culture.

She mentioned Erich Fromm's remark that our two main fears are of losing control and of becoming isolated. I keep experiencing these fears every time I make a move, major or minor, and I wonder if I am getting any better in dealing with them. I find myself with the same old struggles every time I am in a new and unfamiliar milieu. In particular, the experience of isolation keeps returning, not in a lessening but in an increasing degree. Becoming older makes the experience of isolation much more familiar —maybe simply because of sheer repetition—but not less painful.

So, maybe the question is not how to cope better, but how slowly to allow my unchanging character to become a way of humility and surrender to God. As I recognize my fears of being left alone and my desire for a sense of belonging, I may gradually give up my attempts to fill my loneliness and be ready to recognize with my heart that God is Emmanuel, "God-with-us," and that I belong to him before anything or anyone else.

And so a new vision of maturity may emerge; not a vision in which I am more and more able to deal with my own pains, but in which I am more willing to let my Lord deal with them. After all, maturation in a spiritual sense is a growing willingness to stretch out my arms, to have a belt put round me and to be led where I would rather not go (John 21:18).

Wednesday, November 25

For two weeks the workers in the tin mines in Huanuni have been on strike to force recognition of their union. Solidarity strikes in other mines soon followed and finally, two days ago, about twelve women from the families of arrested labor leaders went on a hunger strike.

The response of the government was harsh and violent. Many workers were picked up during the night and put in prison, gas and food supplies to the city of Huanuni were cut off, newspapers were kept from circulating, striking workers were fired, and *campesinos* in need of work were sent into the mines. Since it was evident that the workers were not going to give up easily, it seemed for a while that the government was losing control over the situation and that there might be a new coup to break the deadlock. The miners asked the church to mediate. Archbishop Manrique and the Apostolic Nuncio agreed. Finally, a settlement was reached in which all arrested miners would be set free. A government commission will study the issue of recognition of the unions.

Today the Bolivian newspapers announced that the conflict has been solved. Neither the miners nor the government seems to have won. The emphasis during the strike shifted from the recognition of the union to the release of its leaders. The labor leaders will be free, but recognition of the unions will probably be long in coming. The only good thing is that more violence and repression were avoided. The oppressed and exploited miners will most likely not be better off than before. Hundreds of people have suffered terribly during the last few weeks, a suffering that will be kept out of the papers and yet will become part of the quiet and anonymous suffering of this country.

Thursday, November 26

Thanksgiving Day! There is probably no day I liked so much in the United States as this day. I can remember clearly all the Thanksgiving Days I celebrated in the last ten years. It was always a day of being together with friends, and truly a day of saying thanks. In many ways, it struck me as a more spiritual or religious day than Christmas: no gifts, few commercial preparations, just a coming together to express gratitude for life and all the blessings we have received.

great!

Today I miss being in the United States, as do many people here at the language institute. I could feel it at the dinner table and also in the mood during the breaks between classes.

Still, what is important is to be grateful today and to give thanks. I am more and more convinced that gratitude is one of the most sublime of human emotions. It is an emotion that reaches out far beyond our own self to God, to all of creation, to the people who gave us life, love, and care. It is an emotion in which we experience our dependencies as a gift and realize that in the celebration of our dependencies we become most aware of who we truly are: a small but precious part of creation and above all of the human family. On this day we can say: It is good "just" to be human and it is in our common humanity that we can recognize God's love.

Friday, November 27

A psychology of education must exist which describes the up and down phases a student experiences in learning a new language. This week I felt as though I had not learned a thing since I came here. I experienced myself as stuttering worse than ever, as making the same basic mistakes as when I came here five weeks ago, and as still unable to know what people are talking about when they are not talking to me. I also noticed that expressions and constructions that a few weeks ago seemed quite obvious and even simple to me suddenly became real problems again. A small comfort was the realization of how terribly hard the English language is for Spanish-speaking people. Nancy Quiroga made me aware that *una cerveza* (a beer), *un pájaro* (a bird), and *un oso* (a bear) sounded to her all the same in English.

Today is the last day of the liturgical year and tonight at the language school we will have a three-hour prayer vigil for justice and peace to start the advent season. I am happy for the occasion to pray together with the students and teachers. Though our only reason for being together is to become more able to reveal the presence of God in this world, we seldom have expressed this publicly in common worship.

We all know how far we are from a just and peaceful world. Ireland is on the brink of a civil war, Poland is uncertain whether the Russians will invade, Iran is tortured by weekly executions of hundreds of its own people and its war with Iraq, Guatemala is flooded with terror, El Salvador is being destroyed by oppression and civil war, Nicaragua is more and more insecure about its future, the United States is selling arms all over the world, Europe is in turmoil about the increase of nuclear arms on its territory, the Middle East is more explosive than ever, and the peoples of many Asian, African, and Latin American countries are threatened by malnutrition and starvation. The four beasts of which the Prophet Daniel speaks in his vision are running wild over this world.

There is a good reason to pray, especially for us who have come together from all parts of this world to be peacemakers. We know we cannot make peace with our own hands. We know that we are in the service of the King of Peace who one day will appear on the clouds. To him the kingdom, the power, and the glory will be given, and people of all languages and nations will serve him. We know that he will defeat all the beasts and that his power will be eternal and that his kingdom will never be destroyed (see Daniel 7:14). But we, too, are subject to the temptations of this world, the temptations of greed and lust, violence and revenge, hatred and destruction. We are not immune to the powers of the beasts. Therefore we have to help each other to keep our hearts and minds directed toward the Son of Man, so that we will recognize him when he comes and will be free to stand with confidence before him (see Luke 21:36). We have to keep ourselves and each other anchored in his words, because "heaven and earth will pass away, but my words will never pass away" (Luke 21:33). It is on that eternal Word, who became flesh and lived among us, that our hope is built.

It is Advent again. In his sermon this morning, Oscar Uzin said: Be alert, be alert, so that you will be able to recognize your Lord in your husband, your wife, your parents, your children, your friends, your teachers, but also in all that you read in the daily papers. The Lord is coming, always coming. Be alert to his coming. When you have ears to hear and eyes to see, you will recognize him at any moment of your life. Life is Advent; life is recognizing the coming of the Lord.

In Bolivia the Advent symbols are different from those I am used to. In the past, Advent always meant to me the shortening of days, the approach of winter, and the time in which nature became darker and colder until the day of light. But now I have to learn to wait for the coming of the Lord while spring becomes summer and the light increases day by day. Now Advent means the coming of hot days with their fertile showers. Now Advent is the time during which schools are closed and children play on the streets. Now Advent means a time of blossoming trees and first fruits. And so the symbols of Easter become symbols of Christmas. Maybe my first Advent in the southern part of our planet will reveal to me new things about the mystery of God's becoming flesh among us. Until now, nature has only told me half of the story of God's incarnation; now the other half can be told.

But I have to listen, quietly, patiently, and with inner expectation. Nature can only tell me its other half of the story when I am ready to hear it, when my heart is not so full of false images and unnecessary preoccupations that there is no place left to receive the good news I have not yet heard.

Still I keep making my mistakes. Tonight I went with Richard and Theresa to *The Stuntman,* a movie about the making of a film. The movie was so filled with images of greed and lust, manipulation and exploitation, fearful and painful sensations, that it filled all the empty spaces that could have been blessed by the spirit of Advent. The film showed me how human beings are willing to waste their money, time, energy, and most precious intellectual and emotional talents to create a product that will fill the eyes and ears of thousands of people with images that can only damage the gentleness that lies dormant in our innermost being and asks to be awakened by a Divine touch.

Why did I go to this spectacle with Richard and Theresa? Richard is a kind Englishman who just returned from years of work with cooperatives in Africa, and Theresa is an Australian woman with great interest in music and handicrafts. Both hope to work together in Latin America and come to know better the beauty of this land and its people.

To be together, why did we need this violent and intrusive film? We could have spent our time so much better listening to each other's stories than watching the stuntman's tricks. Why do we keep missing the most obvious signs of God's coming and allow our hearts to be filled with all those things that keep suggesting, not that the Lord is coming, but that nothing will happen unless we make it happen.

I hope and pray that Advent will not be filled with stuntmen, but with the Spirit of him who invites us to listen carefully to the sounds of the New Earth that are manifesting themselves in the midst of the old.

Monday, November 30

St. Ignatius of Loyola was converted by reading the lives of the saints. I can understand this quite well, because everytime I read the life of a saint I experience a powerful call to conversion. Every man or woman who lives the Christian life to the full cannot but exercise a deep influence on everyone he or she meets. What continues to fascinate me is that those whose whole mind and heart were directed to God had the greatest impact on other people, while those who tried very hard to be influential were quickly forgotten.

When I met Mother Teresa in Rome, I saw immediately that her inner attention was focused constantly on Jesus. It seemed that she saw only him and through him came to see the poorest of the poor to whom she has dedicated her life. She never answers the many psychological and socioeconomic questions brought to her on the level they are raised. She answers them with a logic, from a perspective, and in a place that remains unfamiliar to most of us. It is a divine logic, a divine perspective, a divine place. That is why many find her simplistic, naive, and out of touch with the "real problems." Like Jesus himself, she challenges her listeners to move with her to that place from where things can be seen as God sees them.

When I explained to her all my problems and struggles with elaborate details and asked for her insights, she simply said: "If you spend one hour a day in contemplative prayer and never do anything which you know is wrong, you will be all right." With these words she answered none as well as all of my problems at the same time. It was now up to me to be willing to move to the place where that answer could be heard.

All these thoughts have come to me since I have been reading Boniface Hanley's book *Ten Christians.* In this book, Hanley offers simple but penetrating portraits of Pierre Toussaints, Damien de Veuster, Frederic Ozanam, Maximilian Kolbe, Teresa of Calcutta, St. Francis of Assisi, St. John Bosco, Rose Hawthorne Lathrop, Joseph Cardinal Cardijn, and St. Thérèse of Lisieux.

Reading these short biographies is like stepping out of this world and back into it again under the guidance of these concrete human beings. They all are much like me, but also different. They all know the struggles I know, but they are living with them in a different way. They all loved the world, but it was a world they came to see through God's eyes.

After having read such biographies, Ignatius could no longer continue his old life. He had seen how he could live when he was willing to take the risk of total surrender to the love of God.

3.

A Land of Martyrs

Tuesday, December 1

Living with the Quiroga family has helped me understand the struggle of Bolivian life. Every day I see more pain and tears under the surface of this seemingly happy and successful family. A few days ago, Nancy told me that little Rodolfito was not their biological son, but their adopted child. After her miscarriage, Nancy and Rodolfo wanted to adopt a child; but in Bolivia this is not easy. Nancy mentioned her desire to one of her ham radio friends, a medical doctor from another Latin American country with whom she had regular radio contacts. One day he told her that he knew of a little baby boy who needed caring parents. Nancy and Rodolfo went to visit the doctor and took the little boy home.

In Bolivia, however, having an adopted child, or being one, is looked down on as something unusual and strange. Soon Nancy and Rodolfo became fearful that their enemies would use their knowledge of the adoption to harm them. Their greatest concern was that the boy would find out from hostile people that he was not his parents' real child. They wanted to be sure that they themselves would explain to their son how and why they adopted him. This was the main reason for which Nancy and Rodolfo left the country and settled with their son in Miami, to give the boy a peaceful and quiet youth. Only when Rodolfito was old enough to understand that he had a truly safe home and that he was chosen by his parents out of love did they return to their country.

Their return did not bring them the peace they desired. Since their enemies had not left, they soon were exposed to the attack and imprisonment I wrote about on November twenty-third. Although Nancy and Rodolfo clearly want to live in their own country, I doubt that they will do so for long. Their son was so Americanized during his six years in the United States that he not only prefers hamburgers, french fries, soft drinks, and pancakes above anything Bolivian, but also dreams about a future in the land of his childhood memories.

All these things—the intense dedication to the short-wave radio, the six years in the United States, the nighttime intrusion of the paramilitary forces, the boy's fear of being away from his parents and Nancy and Rodolfo's intense concern for the well-being of their son—seem to fit together like the pieces of a strange puzzle.

Wednesday, December 2

"A shoot shall sprout from the stump of Jesse, and from his roots a bud shall blossom. The spirit of the LORD shall rest upon him . . ." (Isa. 11:1–2).

These words from last night's liturgy have stayed with me during the day. Our salvation comes from something small, tender, and vulnerable, something hardly noticeable. God, who is the Creator of the Universe, comes to us in smallness, weakness, and hiddenness.

I find this a hopeful message. Somehow, I keep expecting loud and impressive events to convince me and others of God's saving power; but over and over again, I am reminded that spectacles, power plays, and big events are the ways of the world. Our temptation is to be distracted by them and made blind to the "shoot that shall sprout from the stump."

When I have no eyes for the small signs of God's presence—the smile of a baby, the carefree play of children, the words of encouragement and gestures of love offered by friends—I will always remain tempted to despair.

The small child of Bethlehem, the unknown young man of Nazareth, the rejected preacher, the naked man on the cross, *he* asks for my full attention. The work of our salvation takes place in the midst of a world that continues to shout, scream, and overwhelm us with its claims and promises. But the promise is hidden in the shoot that sprouts from the stump, a shoot that hardly anyone notices.

I remember seeing a film on the human misery and devastation brought by the bomb on Hiroshima. Among all the scenes of terror and despair, emerged one image of a man quietly writing a word in calligraphy. All his attention was directed to writing that one word. That image made this gruesome film a hopeful film. Isn't that what God is doing? Writing his Word in the midst of our dark world?

Thursday, December 3

Tonight we celebrated the first anniversary of the martyrdom of Ita Ford, Maura Clark, Jean Donovan, and Dorothy Kazel, the American churchwomen who were raped, tortured, and murdered in El Salvador. Many sisters and priests from the United States, along with their Bolivian and American friends, came together in the parish church of Cala Cala to pray for their sisters who died such a violent and cruel death. It was a moving service in which faith and hope dominated the sadness about the tragic loss.

For me, the most moving part of the service was the reading of the martyrology by Father Jon Sobrino, one of the leading theologians in Latin America. He lives in El Salvador and is deeply involved in the struggle of the Church there. With restraint, he called out the names of the men and women who have been murdered in Latin America during the last decade. As he let the years pass in front of our minds, the numbers of martyrs increased. And every time he finished the list of victims of one particular year, all the people in church responded with a loud: *"Presente."* Yes, indeed, those who had given their lives for the liberation of the poor were still present in the minds and hearts of the people they came to serve. As the list of names grew—1971, 1972, 1973 . . . until 1981—the word *presente* became louder and clearer.

As I listened I realized that Ita, Maura, Dorothy, and Jean were just a few in the growing number of Christians who died as witnesses for the suffering Christ in Latin America. Hundreds and thousands of men and women in El Salvador, Guatemala, Nicaragua, Chile, Argentina, Brazil, Bolivia, as well as in the other countries of Central and South America, have died violent deaths during the last decade—and, for the most part, we do not even know their names. It suddenly struck me that with the thousands of Latin Americans who died, there are few with Anglo-Saxon names. The courage of those few North Americans who came to live and die with their brothers and sisters in South and Central America is a hopeful reminder that God's love transcends all human-made boundaries.

After last night's service in memory and honor of the martyrs of El Salvador, Jon Sobrino came to the language school for an informal discussion.

There were about fifteen people sitting in a circle listening to Jon's story. Seldom have I heard a story that touched me so deeply. Most of the facts he told I had heard about at one place or another, and most of the explanations he offered were familiar to me. But to hear the story of the horrendous suffering of the Salvadoran people, told by a man who witnessed it all and was involved in the struggle, is an experience that cannot be compared to reading news reports.

The first thing Jon Sobrino did was simply to state the facts. He kept stressing how tempting it is to deny the truth, to deal with it only partially or to present it in a soft way. We need to face the truth of the mass murders that destroy the lives of thousands of civilians, men, women, and children; of the indiscriminate killings to terrorize the poor; and of the selective and well-planned elimination of the leaders of the opposition, whether they are church leaders or political leaders. At least thirty thousand people have been killed in El Salvador during the last two years, and this is a conservative estimate.

The Church in El Salvador is far from united in the face of these barbarities. Jon Sobrino worked closely with Archbishop Oscar Romero, and now he is in close touch with his successor, Acting Bishop Arturo Rivera y Damas. He spoke with great love and sympathy about these men, but left no doubt that they were exceptions. Most of the Salvadoran bishops show little sympathy for Romero's prophetic behavior, which cost him his life. The people might revere him as a saint, but his fellow bishops certainly do not. When some people asked one of the bishops to protest against the torture of one of his priests, he said: "I cannot do this, since he is not tortured as a priest but as a leftist." This bishop is also *vicarius castrensis,* army bishop, and continued to be present as the Church's representative at military functions.

Hearing this, I felt a profound sadness. It is precisely this inner division of the Church that makes a united confrontation of the powers of evil so hard.

I asked Jon Sobrino to say a little more about himself. "Why are you still alive?" I asked. He confessed that his international notoriety was probably his best safeguard. "The military resent deeply all the publicity around their actions in the international press. I am the only theologian of El Salvador who is known outside the country, and my death would create more problems than it would solve. The great indignation in the United States that followed the death of the four American women in December 1980 was very embarrassing to them. They do not want to see this repeated."

Jon Sobrino encouraged me to come to El Salvador and visit his community. "We won't have much time for you," he said, "because there are fewer and fewer priests and sisters to do the work that needs to be done. But we certainly appreciate visits from foreigners, because it is a way of being protected."

I was impressed by Jon Sobrino. His directness, his honesty, his deep faith, his fidelity to the Church, and his great openness to everyone who shows interest in the Church of El Salvador were signs of hope. But the many tensions of the last years have also wounded him. He told us, "People often speak about the beautiful and spiritual victory of the martyrs in El Salvador, but don't forget that the Church in El Salvador is systematically being destroyed and nobody knows how it will end. The only thing we have is our naked hope."

Saturday, December 5

This morning Sister Fran, a Maryknoll Sister who has lived in Bolivia for many years, invited me to celebrate the Eucharist for the blind people with whom she works regularly. With ten blind women and one blind man, we sat in a circle around a table. The first two readings and the responsory psalms were read by the women from their braille sheets, which Fran had prepared for them. After the Gospel reading, there was a lively discussion about baptism and confirmation in response to the story about the baptism of John and the baptism of Jesus. We sang to the accompaniment of an accordian. We listened to words about

God's love spoken by those who have inner eyes. Their faith gave me strength and comfort. "Happy the pure in heart: they shall see God" (Matt. 5:8).

Monday, December 7

After seven weeks at the language institute, I am distressed at how superficial the interaction between students and teachers remains. Maybe this is just my own feeling, but I have not experienced an increase in community between the people at the institute. The atmosphere is pleasant, friendly, and mostly sympathetic, but it is clear that everyone has his or her own agenda and thinks primarily about what lies beyond the institute. Students come to learn a new language as quickly as possible and then move on to the "real thing." In that sense, the institute is very much like a seminary where students endure their studies in order to enter the professional world.

I experienced it in my own seminary years and saw it at Notre Dame, at the North American College, at Yale Divinity School, and at many other places. Everywhere there was the tendency to live, act, and think as if the real life is not here but there, not now but later. This tendency makes the formation of community so difficult, if not impossible. Community develops where we experience that something significant is taking place *where we are.* It is the fruit of the intimate knowledge that we are together, not because of a common need—such as to learn a language—but because we are called together to help make God's presence visible in the world. Only to the degree that we have this knowledge of God's call can we transcend our own immediate needs and point together to him who is greater than these needs.

I do not know if I will be alive tomorrow, next week, or next year. Therefore today is always more important than tomorrow. We have to be able to say each day, "This is the day the Lord has made, let us rejoice and be glad." If we all would die on the last day of our language training, nobody should have to say, "I wasted my time." The language training itself should have enough inner validity to make its usefulness secondary.

There are people from all over the world at this school, and together we represent a treasure house of knowledge, experience, human struggle, and, most of all, of faith, hope, and love. If these mental and spiritual talents could be brought into the light we all would have a beautiful space in which our life together could become an ongoing expression of worship and gratitude. Indeed, we could then experience the kingdom of God among us and thus find the strength to go out to serve people in pain.

But our own fears, insecurities, anxieties, and suspicions continue to interfere with our vocation and push us into small cliques of people in which we find some alleviation of our inner tensions. We quickly fall into the temptation of gossip and divisive words and actions, and before we know it we are imitating all the patterns of the world that we want to change by our ministry. This is the irony and tragedy of most theological and ministerial education. It is therefore not surprising that few will find "out there" what they could not find "right here."

Tuesday, December 8

During the celebration of the Eucharist in honor of the Immaculate Conception of Mary, the mother of God, Sister Lourdes offered a moving meditation. She helped me see Mary through the eyes of the poor people of the third world. Mary experienced uncertainty and insecurity when she said yes to the angel. She knew what oppression was when she didn't find a hospitable place to give birth to Jesus. She knew the sufferings of the mothers who see their children being thrown in the air and pierced by bayonets; she lived as a refugee in a strange land with a strange language and strange customs; she knew what it means to have a child who does not follow the regular ways of life but creates turmoil wherever he goes; she felt the loneliness of the widow and the agony of seeing her only son being executed. Indeed, Mary is the woman who stands next to all the poor, oppressed, and lonely women of our time. And when she continues to speak to people it is the simple and the poor to whom she appears: Juan Diego, the simple old Mexican Indian of Guadalupe; Bernadette, the poor sickly girl in Lourdes; Lucia, Jacinta, and Francesco, the unspectacular children in Fatima.

Every word in Scripture about Mary points to her intimate connection with all who are forgotten, rejected, despised, and pushed aside. She joyfully proclaims: "He has cast down the mighty from their thrones, and has lifted up the lowly. He has filled the hungry with good things, and the rich he has sent away empty" (Luke 1:52–53). These words today have taken on so much power and strength that, in a country like El Salvador, they are considered subversive and can lead to torture or death. Mary is the mother of the living, the new Eve, the woman who lives deeply in the heart of the Latin American people. She gives hope, inspires the fight for freedom, and challenges us to live with an unconditional trust in God's love.

Wednesday, December 9

Psalm 42 remains a source of strength to me. I prayed this psalm many, many times while my mother was dying, and every time since that week in October 1978 it has returned to me in times of distress.

> Like the deer that yearns
> for running streams,
> so my soul is yearning
> for you, my God . . . .
> Why are you cast down my soul,
> Why groan within me?
> Hope in God; I will praise him still,
> my savior and my God.

When I read this psalm last Monday during my morning prayer, I noticed that the psalm-prayer that followed it entered into my soul with an unusual power, so much so that it has stayed with me during the last few days. The prayer says:

> Father in heaven, when your strength takes possession of us we no longer say: Why are you cast down, my soul? So now that the surging waves of our indignation have passed over us, let us feel the healing calm of your forgiveness. Inspire us to yearn for you always, like the deer for running streams, until you satisfy every longing in heaven.

The words "let us feel the healing calm of your forgiveness" are words that I want to hold onto, because if I desire anything, it is the healing calm of God's forgiveness. The longer I live, the more I am aware of my sinfulness, faithlessness, lack of courage, narrow-mindedness; the more I feel the surging waves of greed, lust, violence, and indignation roaring in my innermost self. Growing older has not made life with God easier. In fact, it has become harder to experience his presence, to feel his love, to taste his goodness, to touch his caring hands. Oh how much do I pray that he will let me know through all my senses that his love is more real than my sins and my cowardice, how much do I want to see the light in darkness, and how much do I wait for the day that he will order the surging waves to calm down, and how much do I wait to hear his voice, which says: "Why are you afraid, man of little faith? I am with you always."

Friday, December 11

Every morning at 6:45 I go to the small convent of the Carmelite Sisters for an hour of prayer and meditation. I say "every morning," but there are exceptions. Fatigue, busyness, and preoccupations often serve as arguments for not going. Yet without this one-hour-a-day for God, my life loses its coherency and I start experiencing my days as a series of random incidents and accidents.

My hour in the Carmelite chapel is more important than I can fully know myself. It is not an hour of deep prayer, nor a time in which I experience a special closeness to God; it is not a period of serious attentiveness to the divine mysteries. I wish it were! On the contrary, it is full of distractions, inner restlessness, sleepiness, confusion, and boredom. It seldom, if ever, pleases my senses. But the simple fact of being for one hour in the presence of the Lord and of showing him all that I feel, think, sense, and experience, without trying to hide anything, must please him. Somehow, somewhere, I know that he loves me, even though I do not feel that love as I can feel a human embrace, even though I do not hear a voice as I hear human words of consolation, even though I do not see a smile as I can see a human face. Still the Lord speaks to me, looks at me, and embraces me there, where I am still unable to notice it. The only way I become aware of his presence is in that remarkable desire to return to that quiet chapel and be there without any real satisfaction. Yes, I notice, maybe only retrospectively, that my days and weeks are different days and weeks when they are held together by these regular "useless" times. God is greater than my senses, greater than my thoughts, greater than my heart. I do believe that he touches me in places that are unknown even to myself. I seldom can point directly to these places; but when I feel this inner pull to return again to that hidden hour of prayer, I realize that something is happening that is so deep that it becomes like the riverbed through which the waters can safely flow and find their way to the open sea.

Saturday, December 12

Today we celebrated with Sister Lourdes and Sister Martha the 150th anniversary of the Sisters of Mercy. It was an important celebration for me, since it reminded me of the fact that "the preferential option for the poor," about which we speak so much today in the missionary circles of Latin America, is nothing new and original.

A reading from *Trinity*, by Leon Uris, offered a vivid description of the hunger, illness, misery, and agony of the Irish people in the year 1831, the year in which Catherine McAuley founded the Sisters of Mercy. Catherine's main purpose in those days was to assist the poor, the ill, and the dying, and offer some relief to the victims of Ireland's famine. To help the poor, and preferably the poorest of the poor, is not an invention of Mother Teresa nor a new idea that has been propagated by the church of Latin America since Medellin or Puebla. This call has lived in the heart of the Church ever since the Lord died in total poverty on the cross. Time and time again this call is revitalized and lived out in new ways. St. Basil heard this call when he organized communities to work for the sick and the poor in the fourth century. St. Francis heard this call in the thirteenth century, St. Vincent de Paul heard it in the sixteenth century, and many others have heard it since.

It was good to realize that the Sisters of Mercy, who now form the largest English-speaking congregation of religious women in the world, find their origin in Catherine McAuley's desire to serve the poorest of the poor. Her fervent hope was to make God's mercy visible to the people by simple, direct, and efficient service to those in need.

No congregation today attracts as many people as the Missionaries of Charity of Mother Teresa, who is for the twentieth century what Catherine McAuley was for the nineteenth, St. Vincent de Paul for the sixteenth, St. Francis for the thirteenth, and St. Basil for the fourth century. Every time we see the crucified Lord again in the wretched of our cities, in the refugee camps, and on the desolated deserts and plains of our world, our faith becomes new again.

Sunday, December 13

Newspapers and radio broadcasts are all announcing the frightening news that the government of Poland has declared a state of martial law. The leaders of Solidarity, Poland's new labor movement, have been arrested; churches, cinemas, and theaters closed; people cannot leave their houses during most hours of the day; the military controls the streets of Warsaw; telephone, radio, and television communications have been broken off; and the whole country lives anxiously awaiting what will come next.

Will the Russians invade? What will be the response of China and the United States? Will the people of Poland rise up in protest? Will this be the beginning of a long suffering of the Polish people or even of many peoples? Will this be the beginning of the third World War?

I saw Peter, the young Polish priest, for a moment. He was nervous, tense, and especially angry at the Communists who without hesitation had accused Solidarity and the Church of causing all the problems. He realized that he was excluded, that he would not be able to call his family, to hear any reliable news, or to get any idea about the fate of his many Polish friends. How powerless and isolated he must feel.

I pray that we all will be able to know what God wants us to do in the midst of this increasing tension and anxiety. I pray for Peter and his people, I pray for John Paul II, to whom many look for leadership in this critical moment, and I pray that we will be faithful to Our Lord and to each other in this hour of darkness.

Monday, December 14

Today is the feast of St. John of the Cross, the sixteenth-century Spanish mystic who speaks to me with great power. Not only did St. John experience oppression, humiliation, and imprisonment in his attempts to reform the Carmelite Order, but in the midst of his agony he experienced God's love as a purifying flame and was able to express this love in the most profound mystical poetry.

St. John reveals the intimate connection between resistance and contemplation. He reminds us that true resistance against the powers of destruction can be a lifelong commitment only when it is fed by an ardent love for the God of justice and peace. The ultimate goal of true resistance is not simply to do away with poverty, injustice, and oppression, but to make visible the all-restoring love of God. The true mystic always searches for this Divine knowledge in the midst of darkness. St. John sings "the Song of the Soul Delighted by the Knowledge of God" *(el cantar del alma que se huelga de conocer a Dios).* He sings this song "though it is night" *(aunque es noche).*

In the midst of our darkness—darkness in Poland, Ireland, Afghanistan, Iran, and in most Latin American countries; darkness in the broken, hungry, and fearful families; darkness in the hearts of millions who feel impotent and powerless in the face of the powers and principalities; and spiritual darkness in the countless souls who cannot see, feel, or understand that there is any love for them —in the midst of this darkness, St. John of the Cross sings of a light too bright for our eyes to see. In this divine Light we find the source of our whole being. In this Light we live, even when we cannot grasp it. This Light sets us free to resist all evil and to be faithful in the darkness, always waiting for the day in which God's presence will be revealed to us in all its glory.

Tuesday, December 15
Yesterday, a group of twelve Bolivian workers started a hunger strike in the cathedral. They are asking for a general amnesty for all the Bolivian workers who have been exiled from the country or jailed as political prisoners, for the recognition of their unions, and for the implementation of the human rights guaranteed by the national constitution.

The workers have refused to leave the cathedral to enter into dialogue with the prefect of Cochabamba. Afraid of being arrested, they seek the protection of the Church. A commission representing the prefect is now shuttling between the cathedral and *prefectura,* but so far nothing has been accomplished.

The hunger strikers are supported by large groups of workers. In La Paz and other cities, similar hunger strikes are being organized. The frustration, disappointment, and hostility of the Bolivian workers have been growing ever since the miners' strike. Large general strikes may follow and may prompt violence and oppression by the military regime. Christmas may be far from peaceful this year.

There are many parallels between the situations in Poland and Bolivia. The Bolivian workers have not been able to organize themselves in the way the Polish workers have, but with their determination it is unlikely they will give up their demands easily. In the coming days, the tension and anxiety most likely will increase. In a bankrupt country with a corrupt government, all this will probably lead to more repression, more poverty, and more misery for those who are already close to the bottom.

Wednesday, December 16

Tonight I gave the last of three advent meditations on compassion. During a meeting in November, Ralph Davila had asked for more student initiatives to strengthen the community life of the institute. On that occasion I offered to lead a series of reflections that might be of help to people in their preparation for Christmas.

When I look back at the three meetings, I know that I made a mistake. I should not have offered to give these meditations, but should have stuck to my decision to be a student and not to give any lectures, talks, courses, or presentations during my stay in Latin America. These meditations came forth more from my need to be useful than from any real need existing in the students or staff of the institute.

The three evenings never created any spiritual enthusiasm, and I experienced them in the way I had experienced many obligatory clerical days of recollection in the past, when people came more to please the bishop, the superior, or the speaker than to renew their own spirit. Some few people expressed an honest appreciation; but nothing really "happened." Events like these are little more than ways to maintain the status quo. They do not really help us take a step forward in our committed life together. I have seldom felt so little contact with people as with those who came to these meetings. The fact that Gerry and others expressed their concern that I not let the meetings last longer than the scheduled hour symbolized for me that there was little participation from the heart. As so often happens in clerical circles, obligation won out over desire.

My words remained words coming from far away and did not become life-giving words. I am learning that I am in another world, and that words that can renew minds and hearts at one time and place might have a dulling and even deadening effect at another time and place. I have learned that this is not a time for speaking but for listening; not a time for initiatives but for waiting; not a time to offer leadership but a time to let go of old and cherished ideas and to become poor in spirit. Since we can learn from our mistakes, I might as well use this experience as a way to recall that these are times to be silent.

Thursday, December 17

In preparation for my language classes I had to analyze a short story by the Spanish poet and novelist Carmen Corde. In this story a young mother discovers shortly after the birth of her baby boy that the child is blind. She calls her family together and says, "I do not want my child to know that he is blind!" She insists that from that point on everyone use a language in which words such as "light," "color," and "sight" are avoided. The child grows up believing that he is like everyone else until a strange girl jumps over the fence of the garden and uses all the forbidden words.

I think that this story symbolizes much of our behavior. We all seek to hide what is strange and painful and to act as if things are as usual. We say, "Let us act as if there were no problems, no abnormalities, no pains, no wounds, no failures, no illnesses." In my own life I have experienced the power of this urge to hide, an urge that often is more harmful than what it tries to conceal.

Every time I have had the courage or gave others the courage to face their blindness, their mental anguish, or their spiritual agony and let others become part of the struggle, new creative energies became available and the basis of community was laid. Fear, shame, and guilt often make us stay in our isolation and prevent us from realizing that our handicap, whatever it is, can always become the way to an intimate and healing fellowship in which we come to know one another as humans.

After all, everyone shares the handicap of mortality. Our individual physical, emotional, and spiritual failures are but symptoms of this disease. Only when we use these symptoms of mortality to form a fellowship of the weak can hope emerge. It is in the confession of our brokenness that the real strength of new and everlasting life can be affirmed and made visible.

This was my last day of language school. When I think about my eight weeks of classes, I have reason enough to be grateful. I do not think that there is any better way to learn Spanish than the way the institute has worked it out. Most impressive are the competence, the dedication, and the flexibility of the teachers. Every two weeks I worked with a different team of four teachers. Daily I had two individual classes with sophisticated language drills, one conversation class together with Brian Clark, and one grammar class with a small group of six students. It was a nice balance between intense individual work and more relaxing work with other students. After I finished the three basic textbooks, I asked for more attention for my personal language problems and thus my last two weeks were even more tailored to my needs than the first six weeks.

I was impressed by the way the teachers prepared their classes. They prepared the material of the lessons well, but they also tried to help the individual students with their personal struggles with the language. Ernestina, for instance, gave me a series of special exercises to train me in the use of the different past tenses, and made up many complicated sentences to help me distinguish between the use of *por* and *para,* two words I kept mixing up.

During my short time here I had fourteen different teachers. With this helpful change of teachers every two weeks, I never had a chance to get bored. Different teachers had different styles of working, different ways of expressing themselves, different personal interests, and often also a different way of relating to me. Some were formal and stayed close to the book, others enjoyed little mental excursions. Some used the blackboard a lot and appealed to my desire to see things written down. Others tried hard to train my ear and help me hear Spanish sounds better. Some kept the conversation to familiar household matters; others didn't hesitate to become involved in controversial political, social, and religious subjects. But everyone had something significant to offer and did so with great generosity and dedication. One of the most impressive traits of all the staff members of the institute—teachers, librarians, and secretaries—was their insistence on correcting students on the spot. Since I seldom uttered a sentence without at least two mistakes, I offered them all many opportunities to do their work.

Did I learn the language? I can only say that I gave it a good start, and that another three months is probably necessary to approach fluency in it. On the other hand, I do not have the energy or the motivation to continue at this moment. Eight weeks of intensive training is about as much as I can take in one stretch. I am happy that I am not returning to an English-speaking world but can go to Peru and continue to practice Spanish every day.

If I decide to dedicate a few years of my life to full-time work in Latin America, I probably will have to return to the institute for a few more months of language training. I especially would like to be able to write in Spanish. That certainly would take some extra work. For the time being, however, it seems better to leave the school and let the people of Peru become my teachers.

Saturday, December 19

This morning I went to the cathedral to meet the hunger strikers. I expected that it would be hard to get close to them and to have a conversation, yet I found the church open and unguarded with plenty of people going in and out. In a small sectioned-off area of the large cathedral, the hunger strikers lay on mattresses and blankets, slept, read the newspaper, or talked with visitors and medical aides. During the last few days their number had increased from twelve to forty-eight and about a thousand other workers of MANACO, the largest factory of Cochabamba, had joined them in a separate, supportive hunger strike.

Two men in their late twenties were eager to talk to me. "We are not giving up until the government takes our request seriously," they said. "It is not enough that the government recognizes the unions, we won't stop this hunger strike until the government offers a general amnesty. Thousands of Bolivians live as exiles outside their country since the coup of Garcia Meza on July 18, 1980. We want them to be free to return to their homes and families."

Just a few days earlier, the government had declared that there would be no amnesty this Christmas; but the workers and students in the cathedral made it clear that they would not eat anything until they had accomplished their goals. "Monday our families will join us in the strike if nothing has changed by then. It is going to be very serious."

Meanwhile, aides were walking around giving liquids to the strikers. Sister Mary-Jean, the Vincentian nun from the States who is the newly elected head of the school of nursing in Cochabamba, goes regularly to the cathedral to take the blood pressure of the strikers and to keep an eye on their physical condition. She told me yesterday that the liquid they gave the strikers contained sugar to reduce danger to their health. Nevertheless, the strike is now already five days old, and some of the men are visibly weakening.

"Are you a priest?" they asked. "Yes," I replied. It was clear that the workers had put all their hope in the support of the Church and in the religious sensitivities of the Bolivian people. They said: "The new church (they mean the church that made a preferential option for the poor) gives us much support. Many priests and sisters are on our side and Monsignor Walter Rosales (Vicar General of the Diocese and the highest church authority until the newly appointed bishop is installed) comes regularly to visit us." When I left them they thanked me for my visit and added jokingly: "Write about us in the Dutch papers."

How will Christmas be in Bolivia this year? The rumors are that all the banks will be on strike on Monday to show support for the strikers. Meanwhile, I am struck by the irony that President Reagan offers words of support and sympathy to the Polish labor union Solidarity but refuses any support for the workers in Latin America. The power that criticizes and condemns oppression of the working class when it comes from the Communist regimes ignores, denies, or even encourages the same oppression when it results from the military regimes in Latin America. The issue for Reagan is obviously not, "When are people oppressed?" but, "Who is the oppressor?" The oppressors of the exploitative regimes in Latin America are called "our friends," the oppressors in Poland and Russia are called "our enemies." It seems indeed that the Church today is one of the few institutions in the world willing to defend human rights regardless of who the oppressor is.

The Church is speaking loudly today. Pope John Paul II sent a delegation to Poland to visit Church and government leaders in order to find a nonviolent solution to the increasing conflict. It seems, from the latest newscasts, that the Pope is seriously considering going to Poland himself.

Meanwhile, the bishops of Bolivia wrote a strong Christmas message asking the government to restore the confidence of the Bolivian people in their leaders and to offer a broad political amnesty. "We ask those responsible for the public cause, to restore the faith of the people, which they lost after so many deceptions. The Spirit of justice and true love for the country which transcends the interests of individuals and groups has to be able to return to the people a renewed hope in those who have the responsibility in concrete circumstances. We ask the supreme government for a broad political amnesty, that will open the way to reconciliation of all the Bolivians."

In the midst of all the conflicts, wars, and rumors of war, these strong voices offer hope and encouragement. Although we have to admit that peace and justice have not won the field during the last ten years, we can rejoice in the fact that the voice of the Lord of peace and justice is heard clearer than ever. I pray that many people who are poor and oppressed will find comfort and consolation when they hear this voice, and will find the strength to work together for a better world.

The hunger strikers gave up. Nothing has changed. During the weekend, it became clear that there was absolutely no chance that the government would give in, and that the only possible outcome would be bloodshed and the useless loss of lives. The political analysts, who are trusted by the strikers, persuaded them that the continuation of their hunger strike would only bring misery to themselves and their families.

I tried to understand this sudden change by talking to different people. I concluded from all the comments that the position of the government is so weak that a general amnesty would simply mean suicide for the present government. Bringing the many Bolivian exiles back into the country would change the balance of power so drastically that the present government would have no chance of surviving.

Meanwhile, the economic situation of the country is so bad that any promise to offer better financial conditions to the workers would be empty. Many industries lack the funds to offer the expected Christmas bonus and everyone expects the Bolivian peso to drop in value significantly during the first week of January. The official exchange rate is 25 pesos for a dollar, but at any exchange office I can easily get 35 pesos or more. Meanwhile, it remains impossible for the Bolivians to buy dollars. For those who have debts in the States—as the Quiroga family has—this means a growing financial crisis. Rodolfo bought many goods in the States to sell in his store. Now the Bolivians have no money to buy his articles, and his debts to the U.S. banks increase by the rapid devaluation of the peso. This is a quick way to bankruptcy.

I am sad to witness yet another example of the powerlessness of the poor. The military personnel have large salaries and are allowed to buy goods in special military stores for very low prices. Meanwhile, the poor get less and less for their money and most have to let Christmas pass without being able to give any presents to their children. While the president of the country gives patriotic speeches about love of country, unity of the people, and cooperation between all to save the country from disintegration, it is clear that he and his political friends are protecting their wealth gathered by cocaine traffic and other forms of contraband by giving money and guns to those who are willing to protect their privileged position. The Bolivian army exists not to defend the country against outside invaders, but to defend the wealthy few against the poor and the hungry.

Many of the intelligent people who could provide leadership and change the situation give up, leave the country, and become doctors, lawyers, and businessmen in the United States or in Europe. It is a tragedy that today, in Chicago alone, there are a large number of Bolivian M.D.s while the most basic medical care is lacking in large parts of their own country.

Where is the peace and joy of Christmas? In the United States, in Russia, in Poland, in Ireland, in El Salvador, Guatemala, Nicaragua, or Bolivia? Indeed, "The word was the true light that enlightens all men; and he was coming into the world. He was in the world that had its being through him and the world did not know him. He came in his own domain and his own people did not accept him" (John 1:9–11).

In the midst of all the bad news from Poland and Bolivia, the familiar words from the Song of Zechariah suddenly have an unusual power:

> The God of Israel has raised up for us
> a savior who will free us from our foes,
> from the hands of all who hate us.
> He will give light to those in darkness,
> those who dwell in the shadow of death
> and guide us into the way of peace.

How often have I spoken these words as if they were little more than the expression of an ancient and pious Jew! But here in Bolivia, with the alarming news from Poland covering the front pages of the newspapers, they sound as a call to rebellion, as an invitation to follow a new leader who will throw off the yoke of oppression.

I should not forget that when Zechariah raised his voice Judea and Samaria were occupied territories and that the Jews felt about the Romans as the Dutch felt about the Germans during World War II, and as most Poles feel about the Russians today. Zechariah's song doesn't leave politics behind. In fact, it was difficult for the Jews of Jesus' time to make a distinction between religion and politics. Jesus himself was executed as a political enemy, as someone who claimed to be King of the Jews.

In Latin America, the Good News of the Gospel is a threat to those who oppress and exploit the people. To take the words of the Gospel seriously would mean political suicide for most rulers. The words "God has raised up for us a savior who will free us from our foes" ring out less a note of piety than a call to resistance.

It has been raining the whole day. I had expected a hot Christmas with cloudless skies and a burning sun, but heavy clouds hang over the Cochabamba valley and people walk hastily in raincoats and with umbrellas, jumping over pools of water and trying to escape the splashes of water caused by the fast-driving buses.

I did my Christmas shopping today: two books about jet planes and space travel for Rodolfito, a Spanish metal cross for Rodolfo and Nancy, a brooch and bracelet for Marcelita, and a few things for the Christmas guests in the Quiroga home.

I also wanted to do something special for Christmas. In Rodolfo's store, I had seen little cars and dolls that would make good presents for the boys and girls of the state orphanage I visited last month. So I asked a friend for the telephone number of the orphanage and called the director to tell her about my plan to give all the kids a Christmas gift. The director was very excited about my plan, but when I asked her, "How many kids do you have?" she said, "Seventy-seven girls between twelve and eighteen." Suddenly, I realized that my friend had given me the number of the wrong orphanage. The cars and dolls from Rodolfo's store probably would not please the teenage girls of the orphanage I now was talking with. But I decided to be brave. I acted as if all were normal and promised the unknown director to appear on Christmas afternoon with gifts for seventy-seven teenage girls.

As soon as I told Rodolfo about my mistake and challenged him to be inventive, he and his staff went to work and came up with games, perfumes, mirrors, brushes, and all sorts of other things that—as they assured me—would certainly please girls between twelve and eighteen. On the twenty-fifth we all will go to the orphanage, and I wonder what the response will be.

Meanwhile, I am looking forward to my first Christmas in the summer.

Thursday, December 24

The most important part of this day for me was the celebration of Vespers and Mass of the Vigil of Christmas. At five o'clock in the afternoon, Sister Fran and I went to the small Carmelite convent and experienced the quiet joy of Christmas with the sisters. It was very quiet and peaceful, a simple and restful service. In the midst of the many activities in preparation for Christmas and surrounded by so many political and socioeconomic anxieties, this celebration was a true oasis. The joyful alertness of the twelve sisters offered Fran and me an opportunity to come in touch with the still and deep presence of God in our lives. I read the genealogy of Jesus Christ as St. Matthew gives it in the first chapter of his Gospel. The many names from Abraham to Jesus are certainly not names of saints. They are names of men and women who struggled hard with the powers of evil, sometimes more successfully than others, and who have experienced love, hatred, joy, pain, reward, and punishment, like ourselves. It is these men and women who form the story of which God himself wanted to become part. God, so it seems, inserted himself in our own tiresome and often exhausting journey and became a fellow traveler. When Jesus joined the sad and deeply disappointed disciples on their road to Emmaus and opened their eyes so that they could see what was happening, he revealed what it means that God is a God with us.

God came to us because he wanted to join us on the road, to listen to our story, and to help us realize that we are not walking in circles but moving towards the house of peace and joy. This is the great mystery of Christmas that continues to give us comfort and consolation: we are not alone on our journey. The God of love who gave us life sent us his only Son to be with us at all times and in all places, so that we never have to feel lost in our struggles but always can trust that he walks with us.

The challenge is to let God be who he wants to be. A part of us clings to our aloneness and does not allow God to touch us where we are most in pain. Often we hide from him precisely those places in ourselves where we feel guilty, ashamed, confused, and lost. Thus we do not give him a chance to be with us where we feel most alone.

Christmas is the renewed invitation not to be afraid and to let him—whose love is greater than our own hearts and minds can comprehend—be our companion.

Friday, December 25

Peter, the Polish priest, and I presided together over the midnight Mass in Temporal. Temporal is a section of Cochabamba that does not have its own church. The Marist brothers have a large school there and on Sundays and feastdays they convert their auditorium into a worship hall. Over the years, the brothers have developed quite a parish. Although they have no regular priest, they usually manage to convince one of the priest-students of the language institute to do the fixed parts of the Mass, while they take care of everything else: preparations, music, sermon, and all the details necessary for a good liturgy. The only thing they require of the priest is that he can read Spanish in an acceptable way.

We all gathered on the playground of the school. As I looked out from the steps of the auditorium over the more than three hundred people gathered there, I realized again how mysteriously God keeps calling us together from so many parts of the world. Although most people were Bolivians, and most of them from Temporal, there were brothers from Spain, visitors from the United States, Peter from Poland, and myself from Holland. And while we all are so aware of the conflicts and wars that result from the ethnic and geographic divisions between people, a celebration like this reveals again that God did not create these divisions but wants his people to come together in unity and peace.

This joyful celebration unfolded with mystery and a few surprises, the first of which announced itself as a mechanical bird hidden in the Christmas tree! A large silver ball produced loud bird calls at regular intervals and the layman who acted as deacon during the liturgy was so enchanted with this gadget that he turned it on at the most unusual moments. Just before the Marist brother started his sermon, the deacon walked up to the tree and made the "metal bird" sing its songs. The brother didn't seem to mind. He just raised his voice and competed happily with the bird, who interrupted every second sentence of his sermon with its calls. When the brother invited me to add a few words to his, I first sent the deacon up to the tree to shut the bird up. My Spanish is bad enough; I don't need an artificial bird to punctuate it.

The lights went out during communion, a second surprise. The electricity fails regularly in Bolivia, but this interruption created more confusion than usual. Luckily, many people had Christmas candles with them, and thus we were able to continue and finish the service without many problems. The singing of *"Noche de Paz"* ("Silent Night") by candlelight added to the Christmas mood.

The third surprise—at least for me—was that quite a few boys and girls made their first communion during the Mass. They were festively dressed and looked happy in their new suits and dresses and with their large candles and white rosaries in their hands. I found it difficult to combine the celebration of Christmas with the celebration of the first communion, and to pay sufficient attention to both celebrations during the service, but nobody else seemed to share my problem and thus I tried to go with it as best I could.

Finally there were the *"niños"* (baby Jesus dolls). While celebrating the Eucharist, Peter and I were surrounded by baby dolls, small and large, naked and elaborately dressed, lying on simple cushions or hidden in large glass cases. I never saw so many Jesus-babies together in my life. I soon found out that it belongs to the folk tradition that the baby Jesus has to hear Mass on Christmas day. Therefore families take their Christmas child out of his stable and bring him to church. After Mass, Peter and I were busy for quite awhile blessing all the dolls and giving ample attention to the different ways the baby Jesus looked.

But whatever the surprises were, all the people were happy, joyful, and pleased with this holy night, and everyone went home saying or shouting to each other: *"Feliz Navidad!"* or *"Felices Pascuas de Navidad!"* When I looked up to the sky, I saw a splendid firmament richly decorated with bright stars singing their praises to the newborn child. And we, little people with our candles, rosaries, and dolls, smiled at the heavens and heard the song again: "Glory to God in the highest heaven, and peace to men and women and children who enjoy his favor."

◇

This afternoon we went to the state orphanage, taking with us our gifts from Rodolfo's store. Rodolfo had decided to make his own contribution, and had added to the gifts seventy-seven yellow T-shirts that a Japanese perfume factory had sent him as a form of advertisement. At 5 P.M. Rodolfo, Nancy, Rodolfito, and I drove to the outskirts of Cochabamba and, after a few wrong turns, located the orphanage.

We were greeted with enthusiasm, for the girls had been waiting with great expectation. Immediately Rodolfo began to give everybody in the house one of his yellow T-shirts. One went to a little eight-year-old boy who happened to be visiting his sister that afternoon. Raphaelito was so tiny that I lifted him up and stood him on the table to put on his T-shirt, which went all the way down to his bare feet. With his brown face and big dark eyes staring out from above his long yellow dress he looked like a little cupid. When the girls saw him standing there rather forlornly on top of the table they all began to laugh. At that moment big tears came rolling down Raphaelito's round cheeks and he burst out in sobs. It took us a while to console him, and he needed a few more presents to dry his tears.

What an irony! Here I was trying to make everybody happy and the first result was a tearful boy surrounded by seventy-seven laughing girls. But soon all was forgotten and everyone was excited with the gifts. We talked, sang songs, and played games. When we left we were escorted by Raphaelito and all the girls to the gate and lavishly thanked with handshakes, embraces, and kisses. As we drove away we saw a happy crowd with waving arms wishing us good-bye.

The laughter of Raphaelito and the girls also made us mindful of their unmentioned rejection and loneliness. This joyful interruption in their lives had brought us closer to the sadness of their permanent condition. As we returned to our comfortable home, they stayed in their lonely house; as we are surrounded by the care of family and friends, they wonder if anyone cares.

True ministry goes far beyond the giving of gifts. It requires giving of self. That is the way of him who did not cling to his privileges but emptied himself to share our struggles. When God's way becomes known to us, and practiced by us, hope emerges for Raphaelito and the girls in the orphanage.

Saturday, December 26

At three o'clock Sister Mary-Jean picked me up with her Toyota jeep to take me to the Quechua town of Morochata for the weekend. Her friends Sister Ann and Sister Delia, who run the parish in Morochata, had asked her urgently to look for a priest to hear confessions, to celebrate the Eucharist for the children who were receiving their first communion, and to assist in seven marriages. Sister Mary-Jean, whom I had come to admire as a forthright, courageous, and very lively person, convinced me that to accept her invitation would not only be good for the parish of Morochata, but even more so for me. "You will see fabulous landscapes, you will be excited about the llamas in the high mountains, you will love the people of Morochata, and most of all you will discover what the missionary life is really about." Well, this certainly was an invitation I could not refuse! By three thirty we had left the highway and were slowly curving our way up to the top of the mountains. After a while we could overlook the valley of Cochabamba. What a magnificent view! Dark clouds hung above the city, but the sun found enough space between them to throw floods of radiant light into the valley. As we came higher, we gradually entered into the clouds until we were driving in a heavy mist. As soon as we passed the large cross planted on the top, we could see the clouds breaking and had some glimpses of the little villages below on the other side of the mountain. Mary-Jean drove her jeep carefully through the seemingly endless hairpin turns marked by many small crosses, reminding us of the people who had lost their lives on this dangerous road.

It took us about an hour to make our descent into Morochata. "I am sorry that we didn't see many llamas," Mary-Jean said, "but I promise you will see a lot of them tomorrow on your way back." I hoped she was right.

The priests of the diocese of Dubuque, Iowa, who live and work at St. Raphael's parish in Cochabamba had often mentioned Morochata to me. It was the place where their friend Raymond Herman was murdered six years ago. In different places I had seen pictures of Ray Herman, a young-looking, handsome priest. Why was he murdered? Nobody could answer that question satisfactorily, but everyone agrees that his four years of pastoral work for the poor *campesinos* was the main cause.

About thirty years ago, Morochata was a small, flourishing town. Many wealthy landowners had their houses and managed the *campesinos* from there. The large church and the pleasant central square remind visitors of these old days. There was so much going on in this little town that the rich citizens decided to build a small hotel to accommodate their many visitors. But all of that changed when Victor Paz Estenssoro came to power in Bolivia and initiated a radical agrarian reform in 1952, making the *campesinos* owners of their land and terminating the ages-old system of *latifundios* (large landholdings), on which the farmers were little more than slaves.

Soon the wealthy landowners realized that Morochata could no longer offer them the comfort they desired. Gradually, they all moved away, leaving the town to the poor *campesinos*, who discovered that the land reform did not bring them the promised prosperity. The little pieces of land they now owned soon were divided between their many children. The *campesinos* lack of experience and education, combined with the failure of the government to provide adequate loans for machinery and fertilizer, prevented them from developing a decent economic base.

The hotel, which was under construction when the land reform started, was never finished, and its skeleton only reminded the people of Morochata that their town was once a center of attraction for those who had money and power. In 1971, Raymond Herman came to Morochata to become its pastor. Ray was a diocesan priest from Iowa who had worked for many years in Cochabamba. Hardworking, fully dedicated to his people, concerned for nothing but their physical and spiritual well-being, Ray was as apolitical as one can be, and stayed far from the intrigues that characterize the history of Bolivia. He was deeply loved by his people, by the poor and destitute, and also by those who euphemistically could be called middle class.

When Ray saw the half-finished hotel, he immediately thought: "This should be a hospital." For many years he worked hard to collect funds and find support for his plan, and finally, in October 1975, the building was finished and ready to be opened to receive its first patients.

On the morning of October 20, 1975, the day after the dedication of the hospital, Don Pascual Villarroel, Ray's sacristan, bookkeeper, and teacher of cathechetics, was waiting for Ray to say Mass. Noticing the absence of the jeep, he thought that Ray had probably gone on an errand and would soon be back; but when he found his alarm clock on the ground outside of the rectory, he started to feel very nervous. Finally, he went to Ray's bedroom, knocked on the door, and entered. At first he thought that the priest lay in deep sleep, since he could see only his hair outside the sheet. When he could not wake him up, he carefully pulled away the sheet, and saw an unspeakable horror. Ray had been strangled and two bullets were shot through his head; he had been brutally tortured.

Four hours later, Don Pascual reached Cochabamba to tell Leon, the pastor of St. Raphael, the tragic news. It took him a long time before he was able to say that something demonic had happened.

Don Pascual hardly could say what he really had seen.

The autopsy performed on Ray's body made it clear that the murder could never have been done by one man. A group of people must have entered his bedroom around 2:00 A.M., torturing and killing him. They took the jeep and many things from his room and made it look like an "ordinary" robbery; but if anything is clear, it is that this was a well-planned assassination that had little to do with robbing a priest.

When I saw Ray's bedroom and heard the story, I asked again: "Why?" The answer to that question, summarized from different people's remarks, was: "We don't know. Some people say that the truck drivers did it because Ray was trying to find cheaper ways for the *campesinos* to bring their products to town. Others say that Ray's serious attempt to help raise the standard of living of the poor—the hospital was a symbol of that—had made him the enemy of those who are in control, and that the order to kill him came from very high up."

I asked what happened afterwards. "Nothing really," one of the people said. "Two men were arrested and put in jail, but soon they were allowed to escape. The Bolivian as well as the American governments have covered up the whole event and even today, six years later, nobody knows the true story."

I walked around the church and the little square. The young people sitting on benches greeted me in a friendly way. From the house in which the sisters live, I had a splendid view of Morochata and the mountains that surrounded it. Everything looked so peaceful and serene. But the demonic force of evil had reached this little town too. People knew it. Next Friday would have been Ray's birthday, and people from all directions have come to be sure that there will be a celebration in his memory. He was very much loved; but here those who are loved as he was are seldom destined to live very long. They are reminders of a world that has not yet been realized.

Sunday, December 27

This morning at eight o'clock I celebrated the Mass for Cecilio, Bernardo, Rolando, Linder, and Alejandro, who were receiving their first communion. Well-dressed and well-groomed, they sat in the first pew with rosaries and candles in their hands while parents, godparents, friends, and parishioners filled the church to be part of the occasion.

Most of the boys were twelve or thirteen years old. So the story of Jesus who went with his parents to Jerusalem and stayed there "among the doctors, listening to them and asking them questions," seemed appropriate for the occasion. I enjoyed explaining this story to them, asking them questions about it, and giving them some idea of the great mystery that this Jesus who once was a boy like them, now comes to them as their lasting guide and support in the sacrament of bread and wine. Everyone was radiant, joyful, and grateful; and when the boys came to the house of the sisters for the traditional cup of hot chocolate, they all looked like little princes, even though their real status was more like that of the poor shepherds of Bethlehem.

The weddings took place at ten o'clock. Don Pascual had placed the seven couples and their *padrinos* (the best men and maids of honor) in a large circle around the altar. Since practically no one spoke Spanish, Don Pascual led the service of the word and the whole wedding ceremony in Quechua. I just tried to follow the ceremony as well as I could and did whatever Don Pascual asked me to do.

After the traditional questions and the exchange of vows, some special rites took place. First there was the blessing and exchange of rings. This proved more complicated than I expected, since it took a while to find a finger on which the rings would fit. (Obviously, these rings had known other couples.) Then I took a handful of coins from a plate and gave them to the groom to make him aware of his responsibility to provide for his family. The groom let all these coins fall into the hands of his bride to show her that he would share all his wealth with her, and the bride then flung the coins back on the plate to make it clear that after all money was not the most important thing in their life together.

After this ritual, the *padrinos* put a thin chain around their heads, which Don Pascual then covered with a red velvet cloth. I handed them a burning candle.

Seven times these rituals were repeated. During all of this, the seven couples looked extremely serious; I could not get one little smile from any of them. They had waited in great anticipation for this moment, and for them this was certainly not a moment for smiles or laughter. One couple must have been in their forties. They never had been able to afford a wedding and had to wait many years before they had the money to offer to their friends the fiesta that forms an essential part of the event.

In the Indian culture, no couple will marry in the church without having lived together for some time and without being sure that the woman will be able to bear children. The church ceremony is more an affirmation by the community of their relationship than a beginning of a new life together. When the church becomes involved, the couple has already proven to each other, their friends, and their community that there is a real basis to their union.

What struck me most before, during, and after the event was the lack of any expression of affection whatsoever between the grooms and the brides. They hardly talked to each other; they did not touch each other except when the ritual demanded it. Not one kiss was ever exchanged. Pascual had to remind them repeatedly during the exchange of vows to look at each other, and even that seemed hard for them. When I asked Ann about this later, she said: "Even in their homes, husband and wife seldom show affection to each other, but both are expressive in their love for their children: they play with them, hug them, kiss them, and touch them constantly."

After the wedding ceremony, I celebrated the Eucharist in Spanish and gave to all who were just married and to their *padrinos* the Body and Blood of Christ. Everyone participated intensely in all that took place, even though probably none of them would be able to explain anything about the Eucharist. But their belief in God's presence during this sacred hour could be read from their dark faces.

At twelve o'clock, when I thought that it was all over, Ann said to me: "I have a little surprise for you: there are thirteen little babies to be baptized! Their parents and godparents are waiting for you in the church. I decided to surprise you with it, because if I had told you before, you might not have come!" There was a lot of action and noise around the baptismal font. Every time a baby cried too loudly for Ann's taste, she asked the godmother to give the baby back to the mother, who then immediately gave her breast to the little one. It always worked. Meanwhile, I went from baby to baby with oil and signed their chests with the sign of the cross. Then, one by one they came to the font and, as I poured the water over their heads, they usually protested with loud cries. After thirteen baptisms, we had quite a noisy crowd! But everyone smiled and laughed and showed their gratitude.

"There is one more thing I want you to do," said Ann, when the people had left the church. "There is a lady here who lost her only son of sixteen years last month. His name was Walter. She wants you to go with her to the cemetery, pray with her, and bless the grave." I found the woman sitting on a bench in the village square. As I touched her, she started to cry bitterly. It was a sad story. Last month, Walter went to Cochabamba with a truck loaded with produce and people. As usual, the younger boys were standing on the running board of the truck holding onto the door. At one point, Walter lost his balance and fell from the truck without the driver noticing. He fell between the wheels and was crushed by the back tires of the truck. They took him in the truck in the hope of reaching the hospital in Cochabamba in time, but he died on the way.

Ann and I drove with Walter's mother in the jeep to the small cemetery behind the hospital. There we found the little niche where Walter's body was laid. We prayed and I sprinkled the place with holy water and we cried. "He was my only son, and he was such a good boy," his mother said with tears in her eyes. Ann told me how helpful Walter had been in the parish and how everyone was shocked by his death.

I couldn't keep my eyes from the woman's face, a gentle and deep face that had known much suffering. She had given birth to eight children: seven girls and Walter. When I stood in front of the grave I had a feeling of powerlessness and a strong desire to call Walter back to life. "Why can't I give Walter back to his mother?" I asked myself. But then I realized that my ministry lay more in powerlessness than in power; I could give her only my tears.

At four o'clock, we were on our way back around the many curves, and at five we reached the top again. And there they were! A large herd of beautiful llamas. We stopped the jeep and walked close to where they stood. They stretched their large necks and looked at us with curious eyes. It was a moving encounter, high up in the mountains where there are hardly any human beings. The llamas stared at us, making it clear that we really didn't belong there.

When we descended into the Cochabamba valley, we noticed how the heavy rain had washed away parts of the road. But Mary-Jean kept her jeep on the path, and at six o'clock we rolled into the city again.

I was very tired, but happy. Mary-Jean had been right when she said that I would see fabulous landscapes, would be excited about the llamas in the high mountains, would love the people of Morochata, and most of all would discover what the missionary life is really about.

Monday, December 28

Although the house of the Quiroga family is richly decorated during this Christmas season, and although Rodolfo and Nancy offered a festive dinner to their family and friends, these days have not been peaceful for them.

On the morning of December 24, when Rodolfo and Rodolfito came to the store to start their day of work, hoping that this last day before Christmas would give them some good business, a man was waiting for them with a court order. At first, Rodolfo thought it was a customer who wanted to buy Christmas gifts; but he soon realized that the family member who had sent him to prison last year was trying to do the same again. The hatred of this man must be of a satanic quality; he had chosen Christmas Eve to do as much harm as possible to Rodolfo. The court order contained many accusations; but since most offices are closed on the day before Christmas, and lawyers and judges do not work during these feast days, there was a real chance that Rodolfo would have to go to prison until the authorities could hear his case.

The man who confronted Rodolfo at his store did not allow him to call Nancy or to warn anybody. He and another man took him immediately to the courthouse, leaving little Rodolfito crying in the street with the keys of the store in his hands. When the personnel of the store arrived, the boy told them what had happened. They immediately called Nancy, who rushed to their lawyer; together they went quickly to the courthouse. Meanwhile, other influential friends were informed, and they all soon appeared at the same place to keep Rodolfo out of prison. By noon, things had been "clarified," and Rodolfo could return to his work.

"This is the third Christmas he has tried to destroy," said

Nancy. Although Rodolfo was spared from having to spend the holidays in prison, the whole event robbed him of his inner tranquility and made it hard for him to celebrate freely the feast of Christ's birth. He had to spend much of his time contacting lawyers, witnesses, and friends to convince the court that the whole thing was another attempt of his enemy to destroy his family life, and his peace.

Today the tension finally diminished. Rodolfo and Nancy came home with smiles on their faces, telling me that the lawyers had been able to convince the court that this was a setup without any other basis than personal hatred.

"How can this man get court orders to arrest you?" I asked. "He is very wealthy," Rodolfo said, "and here in Bolivia you can buy anything, even judges and witnesses."

Wednesday, December 30

Tonight I visited the Albergue San Vicente with Gerry McCrane. It is a shelter for young boys of Cochabamba who live on the streets, shine shoes, wash cars, and steal to survive. For many years the Vincentian Sister Anne Marie Branson, who has spent most of her religious life in Bolivia, dreamt about a house where these street urchins could find a home. She felt strongly that this is the type of work Vincent de Paul, the founder of the Vincentians, would have been most interested in. She had seen many of these little boys in the streets in Cochabamba, had talked with them, and had become aware of their dehumanized existence.

Finally, in April of this year, some old buildings and some money became available, and Sister Anne Marie started her new work. She went to the boys and invited them to come to her Albergue San Vicente. Within a few weeks, she had thirty regulars. The boys come in the evening, get a warm meal, receive some personal attention, stay for the night, and go back on the streets after a decent breakfast. The stories of these boys are tragic. An eight-year-old boy was simply thrown out of the house when his mother remarried. He was able to get on a truck and come to Cochabamba. He had been roaming the streets for three years until Sister Anne picked him up and gave him a home. Another boy, ten years old, said: "My mother took me to the market, went to the bathroom, and never came back." Every boy has a painful story to tell.

Sister Anne Marie said: "There must be at least two hundred of these boys on the streets of Cochabamba, but I have room for only thirty. Often the boys come home at night with a street friend, and then I try to give him a mattress for the night. My dream is to build a larger dormitory, so I can help more of these poor kids."

The building where Sister Anne Marie works is simple and poor: one large room filled with beds, a small place to eat, and a kitchen. Sister Anne Marie does the cooking—mostly soup with bread—and tries to help the boys live together in some peace. It is a hard job. These boys are so preoccupied with surviving that they do not afford themselves the luxury of being kind, generous, or peaceful. "The whole world is their enemy," Anne Marie says. "What can you expect? Now they at least eat together without fighting, and I am trying to give them some tranquility and quiet during the night."

As soon as Gerry and I came in, two boys noticed our dirty shoes, pulled out their shoeshine boxes, and gave us a free shoeshine. I was moved when they adamantly refused to accept money for their work. Anne Marie was trying to teach them that some people are your friends and you want to help them without asking for money. "I am trying to get some of them to go to school again," Anne Marie said, "but it is hard for them. They are not used to any discipline, and many of them have so little ego that it is hard for them to apply themselves to any task that asks for endurance. Moreover, it is practically impossible for them to trust anyone. They have no experience of a trusting relationship. For as long as they can remember the world has been hostile to them. I am hoping to get some more professional help, a mental health team, that could assist these boys to develop some confidence in themselves and others."

One boy came in with a bleeding foot. Anne Marie gave him some instructions on how to wash his feet with hot water and disinfectants and how to put on a bandage.

As we walked through the dormitory, a little boy of seven years old stood on his bed neatly dressed in blue jeans and a colorful shirt. He had received these clothes as a Christmas gift and was trying them on before going to bed, because the next day he had to help serve at a dinner being given by some rich people. Eagerly he was looking forward to the occasion.

"Oh, it is just band-aid work," Anne Marie said. "We do not

even touch the real problem, but at least we may help a few boys."

I had heard a lot about the street boys in Lima, and they had often been on my mind. I was happy to see at least one place and to meet one person who had responded to the inexhaustible needs of these children and had shown them that not everyone is an enemy.

4.

In Pablo and Sophia's House

Friday, January 1

Today was filled with packing, saying goodbye, paying quick visits to people to say thanks, returning books, umbrellas, raincoats, and the many other little things that I had borrowed.

At eleven-thirty, we celebrated a liturgy with a few old and a few new students. Gerry McCrane was there with Antonio, his close friend. Happily, Lucha and Albina and the two cooks of the institute also joined. So here we were: five Bolivian women, one Bolivian man, a few Americans, two Irishmen, a Filipino, and a Dutchman. For some, Spanish was their only language. For some, Spanish was a second language. For others, Spanish was just becoming their language. And for a few, Spanish was the great unknown. So we made it a bilingual event with readings both in English and in Spanish and with a dialogue homily and prayers in whatever language the person most easily could speak.

All in all, it was a good last day in Bolivia. I spent a quiet evening with Gerry in his room and felt grateful for his friendship and generous hospitality. As I go to bed I can truly say thank you to the friends in the institute, to the Quirogas, to the Carmelite Sisters, and most of all to the Lord of all people who brought me here.

Saturday, January 2
Lima, Peru

Peter, Gerry, and Fran came with me to the airport to be with me at the hour of departure. Peter will soon start his work in Paraguay, while still suffering from the news that comes from Poland. Gerry will continue to work hard at the institute to make it more and more a center for missionary formation, and Fran will continue to explore pastoral work with the blind and will become an active worker in the parish of Cala Cala. They are three committed people whom I now know as true friends.

Now I am back again in the house where I lived for a week in October. The first person I met was Raymond Brown, the biblical scholar, who is here to attend the Faith and Order Conference of the World Council of Churches. Next week he will come to the house to give a series of talks to the Maryknollers in Lima.

Sunday, January 3

This afternoon I had tea in downtown Miraflores (a section of Lima) with John and Kathy Goldstein. John is a Lutheran minister, Kathy is a nurse; and both are preparing themselves to work as Lutheran missionaries in Cuzco. Our conversation made me aware of how spoiled I am. I am living with a supportive missionary community, well-equipped to help newcomers in getting settled. But John and Kathy had to find their way into a new culture, a new country, and a new type of work all by themselves. They studied Spanish and Quechua in Cochabamba, and now are struggling to find their way to Cuzco. For the last two months, they have been trying to get through all the red tape to obtain permanent residency in Peru, to have their Land Rover fixed, to find good doctors for Kathy (who is expecting a baby in February), and to find an apartment in Cuzco. The months have been very tiring for both, but now it seems that they are ready to move from Lima to Cuzco; Kathy by plane and John with a friend in the Land Rover. Next Sunday, they hope to start their missionary work in Cuzco. "What are you going to do there?" I asked. "We don't know yet," John replied. "It is a totally new place for us. We have to see what others are doing there and see where we can fit in. Kathy can always find work as a nurse, but I, as a pastor, will have to wait and see what is the best way to start a Lutheran mission."

I suddenly realized how lonely they both must feel. Two young people, just out of school, in an unfamiliar country, sent to start a new mission. "It is so frustrating to have to wait so long to get anything done," John said. "Yes," Kathy agreed. "Especially since we are expecting our first baby in a few weeks. It would be so good to have a place that we could call home. Now we live in a small hostel and eat out every night in a different place."

When we said farewell, they said: "Be sure to come to Cuzco to see the baby!" After all I had heard about their struggle, I felt especially eager to celebrate their new joy with them. "You can expect me in Cuzco soon," I said. I feel it is a firm promise.

Monday, January 4

Today Claude Pomerleau and Don McNeill arrived. While I was at breakfast, Claude appeared. I knew he was coming, but somehow he surprised me, as he always does, with the easygoing, smiling way in which he walked into the house. Claude is a Holy Cross priest who teaches political science at Notre Dame University. We have been friends for many years, and whenever there is a chance to meet we grab it. Claude was asked to come to Chile for a month to explore the possibility of starting a Notre Dame extension program in Santiago. He is exceptionally well-informed about the social, economic, and political situation in Latin America. He has been central in the development of my interests here.

Around midnight Don, who heads the Center for Experiential Learning at Notre Dame, arrived. He has just spent two weeks in Chile visiting the Holy Cross Associates, laymen and laywomen who give two years of their lives to work in the missions. Don is a strategist and planner. Without his concrete recommendations and suggestions, I would never have come here. It was he who first suggested that I come to Peru, and he put me in touch with the Maryknoll community.

Claude and Don are close friends, and the idea of visiting me in Peru had captured their imagination. The three of us certainly have a lot to discuss. Yet, more important to me is the awareness of having two close friends who have come to help me start my new life.

Tuesday, January 5

At noon, Don, Claude, and I met Bob Plasker in downtown Lima. Bob, a Holy Cross priest and a close friend of Don's, works with a pastoral team in Canto Grande, a huge *barrio* on the outskirts of Lima.

What struck me most was the contrast between the two forms of ministry to which we were exposed. Bob took us to lunch in Le Sillon Missionaire, one of the most elegant restaurants I have ever seen. It is run by Les Travailleuses Missionaires de l'Immaculée (the Missionary Workers of the Immaculate Mother of God), a community of French women who have similar restaurants in Italy, Upper Volta, the Philippines, Argentina, and New Caledonia.

When we entered, we were greeted kindly by a tall, striking, black sister from Upper Volta who led us to our table and explained a little bit about their ministry. "We want to offer people a milieu where they can taste not only good food, but also something of true Christian hospitality." When I looked around, I soon realized that many bishops, priests, and religious people in Lima come there to enjoy this peaceful hospitality. The surroundings were pleasant. An old mansion with a lovely courtyard had been tastefully converted into a dining space, and while we ate a delicious lunch, baroque music filled the large area and gave us the impression of being transported from the busy streetlife of Lima to a peaceful garden. It was a form of ministry we had not anticipated but Claude, Don, Bob, and I felt grateful for this moment of luxury on our way to Canto Grande.

In Canto Grande, Bob showed us another type of ministry. It took us twenty minutes in a taxi to reach the center of the "desert-city." The word "desert-city" seems the best word to describe this huge new development at the outskirts of Lima; "About a hundred thousand people have come to live here during the last ten years," Bob explained. "Most of them came from the country, lived for some time with friends or relatives in town, and then settled here. You can see the different phases. First they build something like a hut of matted bamboo, and then, over the years, they start earning a little money. They buy bricks, build walls, and slowly transform their huts into small houses. It may take them many years to reach the luxury of a house. Sometimes a fire destroys it all. Fires are especially devastating when there is no water."

I kept thinking about a desert. Yellow sand was all you could see. Trucks, cars, and gusts of wind created a lot of hot dust. The dwellings lacked the two main commodities of modern living—electricity and running water. In front of most houses stone water containers were built to provide the families with washing and drinking water. Large water trucks came daily to Canto Grande to sell water. In many houses there were oil lamps or candles; but most people went to bed with the sun.

Bob and his fellow priests live in a small wooden house in the heart of Canto Grande. It is very simple, but with the help of some plants and a simple rug it looked quite cozy to me.

Bob's understanding of ministry was simply "living with the people, as the people." Instead of a church, he has used different places spread over a large area to celebrate Mass and to conduct other pastoral activities. There was a small pastoral center where the Sunday services are held and where the different work groups have their meeting spaces. The parish committee on human rights is very active and regularly publishes small folders on the rights and urgent needs of the people. On October 20, 1980, this committee, together with many other local groups, organized a march to the center of town to call the attention of the government to the serious problems of Canto Grande: health, energy, transportation, and education. On October 23, the Senate responded and declared the valley of Canto Grande a *zona de emergencia* (emergency zone).

Bob and his fellow workers see it as their main task to work with the people, to make them aware that the Gospel of Jesus Christ supports the poor in their struggle for basic human rights, and to join them in this struggle.

In the short time we were in Canto Grande, we met many good and generous people. They showed hope and a strong will to work for their future. When we walked home through the dark, guided by no other light than the moon, we were grateful to have been able to witness this ministry of solidarity.

Wednesday, January 6

Today Don, Claude, and I did some sightseeing in downtown Lima. One of the churches we saw was the Jesuit Church of San Pedro. A talkative Jesuit brother told us about the busy life of the parish. Daily Masses are celebrated at 7:00 A.M., 8:00 A.M., 9:00 A.M., 10:00 A.M., and every hour afterward until the final mass at 7:30 P.M. "Many people come here," the brother said. "And there are always long rows of people who want to go to confession." While we were standing there talking with the brother, people kept entering and leaving the church. It was clear that at this time of year the main attraction was not the confessional but the Nativity scene, built in one of the side chapels. It was quite a sight. Not only was there the manger with the child and his parents, but around it were landscapes with hills, rivers, waterfalls, and bridges. There were little village scenes with women washing their clothes in the river. There were large herds of sheep and llamas. There were houses in which the lights were going on and off. There were medieval castles and humble straw dwelling places. It was not surprising that many parents took their children there to see the Christmas event laid out in miniature in front of them. But this was not all. In front of a house in which the Angel Gabriel announced to Mary that she was going to become the Mother of God was an American police car, with a policewoman keeping an eye on Mary's house. "We put the car there five years ago," the Jesuit brother explained. "It gives a little touch of modern life. Jesus was born for all people and for all times, and in our time there are many police cars to protect us. We even have permanent police protection for the church." When we looked outside on the little square in front of the church, we saw indeed a white police car and two policemen watching the entrance of the church. It seemed, however, that the police car and the policewoman had not been enough to give the Christmas scene a contemporary flavor. This year a jet plane had been added to fly in circles above the Christmas landscape. By some ingenious mechanism the plane was able to come low and then pull up again, sometimes coming quite close to the shepherds and the Magi, but never close enough to create an accident. "Some people feel that that plane is a little much," the brother said, "but others like it a lot. It is part of our time."

To me it all seemed a little strange, as it was so far from the world of Canto Grande, but it was a genuine expression of the mixture of the Indian, colonial, and technological worlds that underlies the predicament of Peruvian life. Piety and poverty, modern aspirations, realism and sentimentalism, humor and mystery —they all are part of the world of the Peruvian people who continue to celebrate the birth of their Savior.

Thursday, January 7

This morning Claude left for Chile and tonight Don went back to the States. It was good to be together, to deepen our friendship, and to reflect on the new directions our lives are taking. It is strange that after sixteen years of friendship we find ourselves together in Peru, a place none of us thought much about when we met for the first time at Notre Dame. It is a testimony to a radical change of thinking and feeling that has taken place in us all. It is a source of comfort to me to know that in the midst of our inner and outer changes, our friendship has grown. That offers hope for the future.

Four hundred and twelve years ago, on January 9, 1570, Servan de Cerezuela arrived in Lima to open a Tribunal of the Inquisition. My stay in Lima offers me my first direct confrontation with the reality of the Inquisition. The Inquisition in Lima was active over a period of two hundred and fifty years. Artifacts from its history are displayed in the Museum of the Inquisition, which I visited with Don and Claude. It shows large paintings of the autos-da-fé, displays lists with crimes and punishments, shows the dungeons in which the prisoners were held, and has a large torture chamber in which, with the help of lifesize mannequins, the visitor can witness the ecclesiastical cruelties of these days.

The museum, which is the only one in Lima where you can enter without paying, was set up to make a forceful anticlerical statement. The museum guard kept saying to us: "This was the work of the priests." All the torturers were dressed in Dominican habits. In one place we saw a plastic Dominican dismembering a prisoner stretched out on a table. At another place we met a Dominican forcing water into a prisoner's body, thus slowly choking him to death. In another scene a priest was flagellating a man, whose head was locked into a wooden block. Besides these cruelties we were exposed to a vivid presentation of hangings, feet burnings, and starvation, all executed by the "servants of God."

As the guard kept repeating that *"los curas"* (the priests) had done all this, Claude finally responded, "And today the military has taken over their job." He did not realize that just then a man in uniform had entered the museum and heard the remark. The man acted as if he had not heard but said politely: "Good afternoon."

Since my visit to this house of torture, I have been reading about the Inquisition. The evaluation of this shameful episode in the history of the Church varies widely. Henry Charles Lea writes, "The colony was kept [by the Inquisition] in a constant state of disquiet, the orderly course of government was well-nigh impossible, intellectual, commercial, and industrial development were impeded, universal distrust of one's neighbor was commanded by ordinary prudence, and the population lived with the sense of evil ever impending over the head of every one. That there was any real danger to the faith in Peru is absurd. Possibly the Tribunal may have been of some service in repressing the prevalence of bigamy among laymen and of solicitation among the clergy, but the fact that these two offenses remained to the last so prominent in its calendar would show that it accomplished little. In the repression of the practices which were regarded as implying a pact with the demon, the Inquisition may be said to have virtually accomplished nothing. It would be difficult to find, in the annals of human misgovernment, a parallel case in which so little was accomplished at so great a cost as by the Inquisition under Spanish institutions" (Frederick B. Pike, ed., *On the Conflict between Church and State in Latin America* [New York: Knopf, 1964], p. 52).

This evaluation stands in contrast with the evaluation of Salvador de Madariaga, who writes: "the Holy Office of the Inquisition kept its prestige intact with many of the learned, and its popularity alive with the masses, particularly in the capitals such as Lima and in Mexico, where its processions and autos-da-fé were eagerly awaited festivals. The auto-da-fé was above all a pageant of human drama and of colour—human drama because rich and poor alike, when guilty, could be seen under the eyes of poor and rich pass in the procession humbled and crushed under the weight of error and sin; colour because the ceremonies, processions, and settings were carefully staged sights, with the purple silk of the bishops, the black, white, and blue gowns of the monks, the scarlet velvets and blue damasks of viceroys and high officials. . . . The Inquisition was a part of that strange and wonderful life of the Indies, one of the rare periods of History which have succeeded in creating that elusive virtue—a style" (Pike, pp. 63–64).

Lea and de Madariaga are voices on the extremes of a wide spectrum of opinions about the Inquisition. Personally, I see the Museum of the Inquisition as a powerful reminder of how quickly we human beings are ready to torture each other and to do so often in the preposterous assumption that we are acting in the name of God.

Compared with the torture going on in many Latin American countries today, and compared with the thousands of people who have been mutilated and killed during the last few years, the victims of the Inquisition seem few. But the realization that the

Church could encourage and participate in creating ways to cause an excruciating and slow death for those whom it considered dangerous, sinners, heretics, or apostates, can only be a reason for repentance and humble confession and a constant reminder that what we now condemn with strong voices was an intimate part of the Church's daily life only two centuries ago.

Saturday, January 9

Letters are gifts, often greater than the writers realize. Ever since I left the United States, I have experienced a deep hunger for lifegiving letters—letters from very close friends who have little to ask and little to inform me of, but who simply speak about bonds of friendship, love, care, and prayer. I am overwhelmed by a letter that says: "We think of you, pray for you, and we want you to know that we love you." I have never experienced the power of such letters as strongly as during these last months. They directly affect my spiritual, emotional, and even physical life. They influence my prayers, my inner feelings, and even my breathing and heartbeat.

"The Word was made flesh, he lived among us" (John 1:14). These words by St. John received new life for me during my last months here. A word of love sent to me by a friend can indeed become flesh and bridge long distances of time and space. Such a word can heal pains, bind wounds, and often give new life. Such a word can even restore a faltering faith and make me aware that in the community of love, the incarnation of the divine love can be realized wherever we are.

Monday, January 11

Yesterday Jim and Mary Ann Roemer arrived. Jim is dean of students at Notre Dame. He and Mary Ann are dear friends of Don McNeill, and they stopped by for a day on their way from Santiago to South Bend. Today Jim, Mary Ann, and I visited three of Lima's downtown churches. The manifold representation of the suffering Christ became an overwhelming impression. I saw many statues of Jesus sitting in a chair covered with a velvet purple cloak, his head crowned with thorns, streaks of blood covering his face. I saw a painting of Jesus lying naked on the floor, his whole body covered with stripes from the flagellating whip. I saw one altar with a lifesize Jesus figure with the eyes of a man driven mad by torture. It was so frightening that I could not look at it longer than a few seconds. But most haunting of all was a huge altar surrounded by six niches in which Jesus was portrayed in different states of anguish: bound to a pillar, lying on the ground, sitting on a rock, and so on, always naked and covered with blood. All these niches were surrounded by rich golden ornaments—so much so that the whole wall became like a solid gold icon portraying the most abject forms of human suffering.

Men and women from all ages and backgrounds gazed at these morbid Christ figures, some kneeling, some standing, some with crossed fingers, some with their arms stretched out in a pleading gesture. This is the Christ the Spanish conquistadors introduced to the Indians. This is the Christ to whom the people of Peru have prayed during the last five centuries. This is the Christ to whom they bring their own pains and suffering.

Nowhere did I see a sign of the resurrection, nowhere was I reminded of the truth that Christ overcame sin and death and rose victorious from the grave. All was Good Friday. Easter was absent.

I asked a priest about all of this. "Yes," he said. "On Good Friday the churches are packed and thousands of people go to confession, but Easter here seems like a quiet, ordinary Sunday. This is a penitential people."

When we came to the third church, Mary Ann couldn't look at any more. The contrast between the abundance of gold and the tortured bodies of Jesus figures repulsed her. She left the church and waited outside until Jim and I had walked from altar to altar.

The nearly exclusive emphasis on the tortured body of Christ strikes me as a perversion of the Good News into a morbid story that intimidates, frightens, and even subdues people but does not liberate them. I wonder how much of this has also been part of my own religious history, although more subtly. Maybe deep in my psyche I too know more about the deformed Jesus than about the risen Christ.

Tuesday, January 12

At four o'clock in the morning, Jim and Mary Ann Roemer left the house to catch an early flight to Miami. Pete Byrne and I set our alarm clocks early so we could say goodbye. We both felt grateful for their visit and joyful to know them as friends.

This was Ray Brown's day. He gave two splendid lectures on the variety of Christian communities in the post-apostolic period. Ray carefully interpreted the post-Pauline literature (the pastoral letters, the letters to the Ephesians and Colossians, and the writings of Luke) in the morning, and First Peter, Matthew's Gospel, and John's writings in the afternoon. In a convincing and clear way, he presented us with the different styles of the common life at the end of the first century and showed us the various implications for our present-day ministry.

I had to come all the way to Lima, Peru, to hear Ray Brown, who was practically my neighbor in the United States. But it certainly was worth it. Ray made me aware of how much I had allowed the pastoral letters to determine my view of the Church, a church in which structure and good organization dominate. The church life as presented by the other biblical literature—more mystical, more spiritual, more egalitarian—had really never entered into my understanding of the Church during my formative years.

I hope and pray that those who prepare themselves for the priesthood will have incorporated more deeply and personally the different church styles that Ray presented today, and will give hope for an even more multiform life in the church.

Wednesday, January 13

Next week Pete Byrne is leaving for Hong Kong, where the regional superiors of Maryknoll will meet to report on the events in the different regions and to discuss issues of general importance for the society.

In preparation for his trip, Pete called the Maryknollers of Lima together. From this valuable meeting, I received an overview of the variety of missionary activities currently taking place in Peru.

Of most interest to me was the discussion about missioners participating in projects that were cosponsored by the Agency for International Development (AID). AID is a United States government agency that offers financial help to development projects in different countries. Obviously, such aid is given only when the project is in line with the general objectives of the State Department. It was clear from the discussion that Maryknoll did not in any way want its missionary goals to be connected with, or influenced by, the goals of United States foreign policy. Thus a strong statement was sent to the meeting in Hong Kong, declaring that the Maryknoll Missionary Society should not participate in any projects that received money from AID.

This important statement shows a growing hesitation on the part of U.S. church people to be connected with United States government policies. There was a time when being a good Catholic and being loyal to the U.S. government were closely connected. But today, being a Christian and being a loyal patriot are no longer necessarily the same, and the Catholic Church is less and less eager to identify itself with the American "cause." This is clear not only in the Maryknoll statement, but also in the recent statements of U.S. bishops concerning both United States foreign policy in Central America and the nuclear arms race.

It took a long time to move away from the "Constantinian connection," but the Reagan policies have certainly helped to speed up the process of disconnecting.

Thursday, January 14

Tonight I finally moved to Pamplona Alta. I have now been in Peru for twelve days, and I have needed all that time to get oriented, meet different Maryknollers, get a feel for the region, and organize my own affairs. It is good to move away from the comfortable American climate of the center-house into the Peruvian world.

Pete Ruggere drove me in his blue Volkswagen to my new living quarters with the Oscco-Moreno family. They are his neighbors, and with their help he has built a pleasant room on top of the roof of their house. The word "roof" is a euphemism since this house, like many of the houses in the area, is only half-finished. Construction continues at a variable rate depending on money, need, and time. My little room, therefore, might better be seen as the first room built on the second floor. Since nothing else is finished on the second floor, I have in fact a large terrace looking out over the many houses of the neighborhood. My room consists of four brick walls—painted pink ("the only color I had") by our neighbor Octavio—and a roof made of sheets of metal. There is a door and a window, but the wind and the dust have free access to my home since the builders left a lot of open spaces where walls, window, door, and roof meet. With virtually no rain here and with little cold weather, my small place seems quite comfortable and pleasant.

I often have thought about having a *poustinia* or small building for prayer on the marketplace, and this new place seems to be just that. It is like a monk's cell between a large sea of houses and people.

I was warmly welcomed by the downstairs family of Sophia and Pablo and their three children, Pablito, Maria, and Johnny. They all showed great kindness to me, and the kids were soon hanging on my arms and legs.

Pete Ruggere, Tom Burns, and Larry Rich live in the next house. There I can go at any time to wash, use the bathroom, eat, listen to music, or watch television. Their house is a section of the house in which Octavio and his wife and eleven children live. The space looks very small to me, and I wonder where and how they all live and sleep. But last night at ten o'clock nobody seemed to be sleeping. Kids of all ages kept walking in, out, and around, usually accompanied by a few dogs. Everyone is open, smiling, friendly, and obviously quite poor.

Friday, January 15

Today I came to know my new family a little better. I played with Johnny, Maria, and Pablito, took some photographs of them, let them show me the different neighborhood stores, and took them to Mass at night. I also talked a little with Pablo and his wife, Sophia. Pablo works as a butcher in the large market of Ciudad de Dios, and Sophia takes care of the family. The house consists of three dark rooms with walls of gray cement. One room functions as the kitchen, the other as the children's bedroom, and the third serves as living room, dining room, television room, and bedroom for Pablo and Sophia.

From talking with Pablo, I learned that the two most treasured items in the house are the television and the refrigerator. When I came home from Mass with the three children, Pablo was standing on the street corner talking with a neighbor. When he saw me, he said: "Father, we are talking about the robberies on our street. At night, robbers drive their cars up, climb on the roof, and enter the house from above. They are after our televisions and refrigerators. The few things we have, they try to take away from us! It is becoming an unsafe place here."

A noticeable fear could be heard in Pablo's voice. A little later Sophia joined in the conversation, saying: "Can you believe it?

They steal from the poor, those *rateros.''* For a moment, I thought that *rateros* meant "rats," but a rat is *una rata.* Usually *ratero* means pickpocket, but here it is used for thief.

The Oscco-Moreno family is poor, but not miserable. The children are well cared for, seem to be healthy, and are playful. Pablo has a job and seems to make enough to give his family the basics. The television and the refrigerator show that they make a little more than their neighbors. Their daily life is very simple. They seem to keep pretty much to themselves. Johnny is never far from his thirteen-year-old brother, Pablito, and always gives him a hand when they walk together. Maria, who is ten years old, spends more time with her mother. It is a simple, but happy family; but not without the fears and anxieties of most poor people. I do not think they are eager churchgoers, but the walls show many pictures of Jesus, Joseph, and Mary. I am glad to live with these people. They teach me about life in ways no books can.

Saturday, January 16

My home in Pamplona Alta is about a fifteen-minute walk from the church of Ciudad de Dios. When people say, "I am going to the city," they do not mean the center of Lima, but the place where the first invasion of poor people took place in 1954, and where Cardinal Cushing built the large church that is staffed by Maryknoll.

Tonight I walked to the church; and when I got there, I saw large groups of people in the parish office as well as in the church. The office was filled with people who came to register for baptism, first communion, or marriage; and the church was filled with parents, godparents, and children waiting for a baptismal ceremony. I attended the baptisms. At first, I thought that only babies were being baptized, but soon I saw teenagers walking up with their parents and godparents to the baptismal font. When people started to lift up these boys and girls like babies, "Padre Carlos" —the Maryknoller Charles Murray—told them that they could stand on their own feet and only needed to incline their heads to be baptized. Before doing so, however, Charles asked them some questions about their faith to make them aware that they were no longer babies, but could answer for themselves.

After Charles had baptized about twenty babies and children, Pete Ruggere walked up to him and said: "There is a wedding here at seven o'clock, and it is already ten past!" Ten minutes later, Charles had finished the baptisms and the church was again filled with the family and friends of the couple to be married. An hour later, another couple was married and the church filled anew with people. Meanwhile, the staff in the office was busy filling out forms, answering questions, advising about preparation for first communion and marriage, and trying to help with whatever problem came up.

To me it all seemed hectic, even chaotic. But for Charles, Pete, and Tom, the priests of Ciudad de Dios, it was just another Saturday night.

Talking about this seemingly busy parish, Pete said, "There are one hundred and twenty thousand people living in this parish. We reach only about 5 percent of them." There is room for at least ten churches within the boundaries of the present parish. Many invasions of people over the last thirty years have made this one of the most populated areas of Lima, and the long lines of people waiting at the parish office testify to the tragic lack of pastoral personnel and facilities in the "City of God."

Sunday, January 17

This morning at nine o'clock I celebrated the Eucharist in the Church of Ciudad de Dios and preached. Preaching for very poor people is an activity that forces you to be honest with yourself. I kept asking myself: "What do I really have to say to these people?" I had the feeling that they had more to say to me than I to them. I thought: "Who am I to think that I can say anything of value in this situation. I have never been poor, I have never had to struggle with survival as these people have, and I do not even know their language!" And yet I knew that I was here to preach and that none of my hesitations was a valid reason not to preach. That, I am sure, is part of the mystery of being sent. I prayed that somehow God would touch the hearts of the people through my own broken words.

The Gospel told the story about Andrew and another disciple of John who followed Jesus. Jesus said: "What are you looking for?" They said: "Rabbi, where do you live?" When Jesus said: "Come and see," they stayed with him. Later, Andrew shared what they had seen and heard with his brother Simon, and so Simon came to Jesus. This story offers three important verbs to reflect upon: to look for, to stay, and to share. When we search for God, stay with him, and share what we have seen with others, we become aware of the unique way that Jesus calls us. A vocation is not a privilege of priests and sisters. Every human being is called by Jesus in a unique way. But we have to be looking for God, we have to be willing to spend time with him, and we must allow others to become part of our spiritual discoveries. The three Spanish words—*buscar, quedar,* and *compartir*—helped me to articulate what I wanted to say.

I wanted to help the people realize that they are important in God's eyes, and that they are called as much as any other human being. I hope that—in between all my broken Spanish—people sensed at least that I took them seriously, and that God certainly does. But when I am honest, I have to confess that the youth choir with its liberation songs received a lot more attention than I did with my sermon. The powerful songs led by a fervent university student, Javier, seemed in this instance to express the spirit of the people better than the words of a foreigner.

Monday, January 18

Every day I see and hear a little more about the different forms of pastoral care in this immense parish. Today I saw the "parish kiosk" and "the library."

On Monday mornings from 9:00 to 12:00, Tom Burns goes to his little kiosk, which he built in one of the small markets in the parish. This market consists of about two hundred stalls where vegetables, fruit, and cloth are sold, and here people from the neighborhood come for their daily shopping. It is not a flourishing place. Since the vendors can only sell small quantities, their prices are high compared to those of the large market in Ciudad de Dios. Among all these little stalls, Tom has his *kiosko parroquial* (parish kiosk). With a smile, he tells me that his motto is: *"Aqui no se venden verduras, sino verdades"* ("Here we sell not vegetables but truths"). As we arrived at the *kiosko,* people greeted us with big smiles. Tom's first task is to unlock the place and open the wooden shutters. It looks just like a small newspaper stand, the only difference being that instead of buying newspapers, you can enter it and talk with a priest.

The loudspeaker of the market announces that "Padre Tomas" has arrived and welcomes visitors. It was a slow morning. One person came to talk about the first communion of his child. Another asked for help to get his daughter into high school, and someone else had marriage plans to talk about.

While Tom received his parishioners, I walked around the area with Sister Mary Kay, whom we met in the market. She offered to show me her library, a little old medical dispensary that was no longer used as such. "We had the building and wanted to put it to good use," Mary Kay explained. "We wondered if we could make it available to the schoolchildren, who have no books with which to study. We didn't realize that we had struck a pastoral gold mine. We often had wondered how to reach the youth, and we had not been very successful. But when we opened this little library, we suddenly found ourselves surrounded by hundreds of boys and girls eager to learn." It was a small operation, but very effective. Every day after school, the children come, take out the book that the teacher has recommended, and study it in the reading room. No book can be taken home; all the studying takes place in the library itself. The children themselves tell the staff what books they need most, and thus slowly a library has been formed geared to the needs of the children. History, geography, mathematics, and religion were well represented. There also were quite a few classic stories in comic strip form, which proved to be quite popular. The whole collection was kept in a small room and could fit on a dozen shelves, but more than a thousand young people are being helped by this mini-library.

I asked Sister Mary Kay, "How do students normally study?" She answered, "By taking notes in class and studying them. The children and the schools are too poor to have books. All education is note-taking." I asked again: "Was there any way for these kids to read books before this library existed?" "Yes," Mary Kay answered, "But they had to go to downtown Lima and stand in line for hours to use a book for awhile, and very few had the time, the opportunity, and the motivation to do so."

While we were talking, a group of teenagers was having a mathematics class in the reading room. Mary Kay told me, "Many students have problems with mathematics. So, during the summer, we hire a mathematics teacher to help the students catch up. It is a very popular class."

What most impressed me was the great eagerness to learn. Education was clearly seen as *the* way to get out of poverty and to move ahead in life. I could see on the faces of the students how seriously they took their classes. Keeping order was obviously no problem for the teacher.

"We never were fully aware of this need," Mary Kay said. "We have worked here for many years and only accidentally hit on this ministry. When we started this library, we wondered if anyone would use it. Now we have more than one thousand regular users, and we meet more young people than ever before. We are very excited about it."

As we walked back to the marketplace, we heard the loud-speaker announce a course for adults in Peruvian history: seven lectures and a trip to the anthropological Museum in Lima. Price: 100 *soles* (20 cents). "That is one of the courses we have organized. It is quite popular," Mary Kay said.

We found Tom alone in his kiosk reading a book about the Kingdom of God. It suddenly hit me that Tom and Mary Kay had given me a better understanding of Jesus' words, "The Kingdom of God is among you."

Tuesday, January 19

Tomorrow a two-day conference on El Salvador starts in Lima, organized by the Social Democrats. Although they are almost unknown in the United States, the Social Democrats are a power-ful political force throughout Europe and the third world. There are more than seventy social democratic parties, and about twenty-five of these are exercising power—among them, the par-ties of Helmut Schmidt in Germany and François Mitterrand in France. The Social Democrats have nothing to do with the Com-munists, who look at them as nothing more than another form of bourgeois political liberalism.

All of the world's social democratic parties have joined together in an organization called the Socialist International. Under its pres-ident, Willy Brandt, it has made a great effort in recent years to give support to democracy and liberation movements throughout the third world. It supported, for instance, the Sandinista struggle against the dictatorship of Anastasio Somoza. In Europe and in many circles of the third world, the Social Democrats are well known and greatly respected. It is for these reasons that the Lima meeting is so important.

Some members of the United States delegation to the conference visited the parish this afternoon. Robert Drinan, S.J., former United States congressman; Joe Eldridge, director of the Washington Office in Latin America (WOLA); and Larry Burns, the key person of the Council of Hemispheric Affairs (COHA). WOLA and COHA are two highly regarded human rights organizations that work out of Washington, D.C. Regrettably, the visitors did not have enough time to come to my neighborhood, so I missed meeting them. Tom Burns, who will attend the conference as a representative of Maryknoll, showed them a little of Ciudad de Dios and answered some of their questions.

Wednesday, January 20

Can we truly live with the poor? Although I live with them and share their life to some extent, I am far from poor. During the noon hour, I walk to the rectory in Ciudad de Dios and eat a good meal prepared by a good cook, and one day a week I go to the Maryknoll center house in Miraflores to take a shower, sleep in, and have a day of relaxation.

So my living with the poor hardly makes me poor. Should it be different? Some say yes, some say no. Some feel that to be a priest for the poor, you should be no different from them, others say that such is not realistic or even authentic.

I have been here only one week, and thus am unable to have an opinion, but I know one thing: right now I would be physically, mentally, and spiritually unable to survive without the opportunity to break away from it all once in awhile. All the functions of life, which previously hardly required attention, are complicated and time-consuming operations here: washing, cooking, writing, cleaning, and so on. The winds cover everything with thick layers of dust; water has to be hauled up in buckets from below and boiled to be drinkable; there is seldom a moment of privacy, with kids walking in and out all the time, and the thousands of loud sounds make silence a faraway dream. I love living here, but I am also glad that I can escape it for two hours a day and for one day a week. Living here not only makes me aware that I have never been poor, but also that my whole way of being, thinking, feeling, and acting is molded by a culture radically different from the one I live in now. I am surrounded by so many safety systems that I would not be allowed to become truly poor. If I were to become seriously ill, I would be sent back to the United States and given the best possible treatment. As soon as my life or health were really threatened, I would have many people around me willing to protect me.

At this moment, I feel that a certain realism is necessary. I am not poor as my neighbors are. I will never be and will not ever be allowed to be by those who sent me here. I have to accept my own history and live out my vocation, without denying that history. On the other hand, I realize that the way of Christ is a self-emptying way. What that precisely means in my own concrete life will probably remain a lifelong question.

I am writing all this from my comfortable room in the center house in Miraflores, where I have a day off. I enjoyed my shower, I am glad to receive mail and have a dust-free desk on which to answer it, and I look forward to reading a book, seeing a movie, and talking to friends about religion, politics, and "home." But I am also happy that tomorrow I can return to Pablito, Johnny, and Maria and play with them in Pamplona Alta.

Thursday, January 21

The conference of the Social Democrats on El Salvador ended today. Tom Burns, who attended all the meetings as a Maryknoll representative, and Larry Rich, who attended as a journalist for *Noticias Aliadas* (Latin American Press), both felt optimistic about the strong statement issued against United States military intervention and against elections without negotiations. Moreover, a feeling emerged that this conference had created a powerful human rights platform in Latin America.

Friday, January 22

This afternoon Sister Pam and I visited several families with retarded children. Trained in special education, Pam has worked for many years with the physically and mentally handicapped.

Pam came to Pamplona Alta to continue the work that Sister Mariana had started. After many years of patient work, Sister Mariana had built a small school for children who need special education and had identified the families with handicapped children. While doing this difficult and often ungratifying ministry, she herself was fighting cancer in her own body. Finally, she realized that she was losing the battle and had to return to the United States. In July 1981 she died.

One of the consolations during her last months of life was that someone would continue her work. When Sister Pam arrived, she found a well-organized card system with all the names and addresses of the families who needed special attention.

As we walked through the sandy streets, Pam said: "I am only visiting those children who are too handicapped to be able to go to the school." We visited a twelve-year-old girl who is unable to speak, hardly able to walk, and totally dependent for all basic life functions on her mother and two brothers. We visited a little six-year-old boy, one of eleven children, who suffers from cerebral palsy and cannot speak. We visited a three-year-old boy who has regular convulsions and seems to be getting worse as he grows older. We visited an extremely retarded thirteen-year-old girl who, as a result of the dysfunction of her glands, had grown so fat that a huge chair had to be built for her. And so we went from house to house.

All these people lived in extreme poverty. Many of the dank, humid hovels looked worse than stables; they were filled with naked children and terrible smells, and lacked any sanitary facilities. In one house, a four-year-old retarded girl who refused to wear clothes kept ripping off any dress they tried to put on her. She was living naked on a cement floor surrounded by chickens and dogs, making strange, inarticulate noises.

"One of the problems I have," Pam said, "is to get the cooperation of the family in the treatment of these retarded children. It is so hard to convince the parents to do regular exercises with their children and thus to help them in the development of their muscles." I soon saw how right she was. When we visited an eighteen-month-old child with Down syndrome, we realized that the baby always lay on her back and was not developing the muscles necessary to lift her head, to reach out her arms, or to strengthen her legs. Pam said: "I keep telling her mother and older sisters to teach her to walk and to help her lift up her head, but they simply don't do it. Every time I come here, I find the little girl again on her back in bed. As you can see, she is less developed than her five-month-old brother. It is so hard to convince people that something can really be done for retarded children. Parents tend to give up soon and neglect their retarded children. They do not really believe that any help is possible."

My walks with Sister Pam gave me a glimpse of the larger

dimensions of poverty. Poverty is so much more than lack of money, lack of food, or lack of decent living quarters. Poverty creates marginal people, people who are separated from that whole network of ideas, services, facilities, and opportunities that support human beings in times of crisis. When the poor get sick, have handicapped children, or are the victims of an accident, no help seems available. The poor are left to their own minimal resources.

It suddenly hit me how crucial it is for the poor to organize themselves into supportive communities. But for people who struggle day after day just to survive, little energy remains to build these necessary networks.

Saturday, January 23

Pam and I continued our visits today. In one house we met a little two-year-old girl whose face and left hand were terribly deformed as a result of a fire. While the mother was away from home, her bamboo-matted house caught on fire and the burning roof fell on the baby, who was lying alone on the bed. The doctors were able to save the child's life, but they did not perform surgery to restore her face and hand. The mother, an energetic and intelligent woman, went many times to the hospital to ask for further treatment but was sent back again and again with the message that there was no bed available.

Pam said: "When I saw this girl, I realized that a further delay of surgery would make it more and more difficult to restore her face and hand. So I went to a group of wealthy women in Lima who want to help poor sick children and pleaded with them to accept this child. They finally promised to take her on and now I hope that we can find a private clinic where surgery can be done. Without ample financial support, nothing is going to happen."

This seemed to be a typical story. Good medical care is out of the reach of the poor, and many poor people do not even try to find it. Often they do not have the time, the opportunity, or the transportation to go to a good hospital; and frequently they cannot pay for the medicines the doctors prescribe.

Parents simply do not have the time and energy to give the necessary attention to their handicapped child. In one of the houses we found a totally paralyzed three-year-old boy lying on his parents' bed. His little brothers and sisters were playing around the house. Both parents were absent. The father works from 7:00

A.M. to 11:00 P.M. on odd jobs to earn enough to keep his family alive, and the mother goes far distances every day to bring her husband his lunch and to do the necessary errands for the family. When Pam told the mother that she had to do daily exercises with her little boy to help him develop his leg, arm, and neck muscles, she simply said: "I cannot do it. I do not have the time for that work."

In another house, Pam had come across a fourteen-year-old boy, Alfredo, who had had meningitis when he was twelve and had been in the hospital for one year. He was partially paralyzed but had a good mind. Since he had come home, however, he stayed in bed watching television all day. He had become totally passive. Pam said: "It took me endless visits to get the boy to talk, to read, and to do some schoolwork." When Pam and I entered the house, he was sitting in a chair with a book. It was more than Pam had expected. With some difficulty, Alfredo talked with me. Together we read a story about David and Absalom and tried to discuss some of the questions at the end of the story. Alfredo had no difficulties in grasping the content of the story; but I realized that, without constant personal support, he would probably not be motivated enough to do regular homework. With both parents absent most of the time, it is unlikely that he will come far in developing his muscles as well as his mind.

Wherever we went, we came across similar situations: poor, overburdened people unable to give the members of their family the basic help they need and unable to afford the help that is available to the happy few.

Sunday, January 24

Today I became fifty years old. I am glad that I can celebrate this birthday in the parish of Ciudad de Dios and with my family in Pamplona Alta. I hope that by concluding here half a century of living, I am perhaps moving toward a new way of living and working in the future.

There were small celebrations at different moments during the day. Father Charles announced my birthday to the people in church at the nine o'clock Mass, which I celebrated. As a result, I received several hundred kisses and embraces from the people after Mass. At noontime Father John Eudes, the abbot of the Genesee Abbey, and Kay, Eileen, and Virginia, friends from New

Haven, surprised me with their congratulations by phone. After dinner there was the traditional birthday cake with candles, and at 6:00 P.M. I brought a cake to my family to have a little *fiesta* with them. Pablito, Johnny, and Maria sang "Happy Birthday," I blew out the candle (which I had put into the cake myself), and Sophia made some coffee. Together we watched the cartoons on television, and Johnny beat me in a game of checkers.

Later Charles, Pete, Tom, Larry, and I went out for a pizza; and there Charles asked me the difficult question: "How does it feel to be fifty?"

"How does it feel?" It feels quiet and peaceful. I am here with good, simple, and affectionate people; I sense that God wants me to be here; and this fills me with a simple joy. The words of Paul to the Corinthians, which we read during Mass today, expressed my feelings very well: "Our time is growing short. . . . Those who mourn should live as though they had nothing to mourn for; those who are enjoying life should live as though there were nothing to laugh about . . . " (1 Cor. 7:29–30).

I felt a little of this "spiritual indifference." Within a few years (five, ten, twenty, or thirty) I will no longer be on this earth. The thought of this does not frighten me but fills me with a quiet peace. I am a small part of life, a human being in the midst of thousands of other human beings. It is good to be young, to grow old, and to die. It is good to live with others, and to die with others. God became flesh to share with us in this simple living and dying and thus made it good. I can feel today that it is good to be and especially to be one of many. What counts are not the special and unique accomplishments in life that make me different from others, but the basic experiences of sadness and joy, pain and healing, which make me part of humanity. The time is indeed growing short for me, but that knowledge sets me free to prevent mourning from depressing me and joy from exciting me. Mourning and joy can now both deepen my quiet desire for the day when I realize that the many kisses and embraces I received today were simple incarnations of the eternal embrace of the Lord himself.

Monday, January 25

This afternoon Betty Evans presented a lecture on the history of Peru, the first in a mini-course offered to the women of Pamplona Alta and organized by the women's commission of the Center of the People's Culture.

Betty Evans—a Peruvian teacher married to an Englishman—gave a lively presentation with slides about the formation of the Inca culture in Peru. The thirty or so women, who had come from different sections of Pamplona Alta to the public soup kitchen in the little market where Tom has his kiosk, showed great interest in Betty's talk and a strong desire to learn about their own past. Some came because their children had questions they couldn't answer, others because they simply felt a need to know more about their own history. Everyone came to meet other women and to become aware of common interests, needs, and roots. Betty designed the course to help the women understand better why they live the way they live, and what factors have played a role in the development of their present socioeconomic situation.

After the lecture, Mary Kay told me that when the children were asked to draw pictures of their families, many depicted the father drunk or fighting, and the mother doing all the heavy work. Mary Kay said: "Betty is going to talk with these children to get a better idea of the way they experience their parents." I began to see how a course for women about their own history could be an important tool in the slow process of human liberation.

Wednesday, January 27

Anyone who has lived awhile in one of the poor sections of Lima tends to warn visiting friends against robbers and pickpockets. "Do not wear your watch visibly on the bus, someone will rip it off;" "Be sure to have a second pair of glasses, someone might pull your glasses from your head to sell the frame;" "Do not let your purse hang loosely from your shoulders, someone might cut the straps and run away with all your money and your papers;" and so on. Such warnings can be heard every day, often coupled with dramatic stories to show that the warnings are necessary.

Today, however, I heard a story about the consequences not of carelessness but of hypervigilance. A nun who had lived in Lima for quite some time had a friend visiting her. One afternoon, when this friend wanted to go shopping in the market, her experienced host said: "Now, be careful on the buses and in the market place. Before you know it, they will grab your money, your purse, and your watch. Be sure to take your watch off and put it in your purse and hold your purse tight under your arm."

Thus warned, the sister went on her way. The bus was crowded as always, and she had to push her way into it, always conscious of the potential robbers around her. While the bus was moving, and the sister was holding on to the handle to keep her balance, she suddenly noticed her watch on the bare arm of a young man leaning against her.

Overcome by the awareness that after all the warnings she had not been able to avoid being robbed, and furious at the shameless thief, she screamed: "You stole my watch, give it back immediately." While saying this, she pulled out her pen and pushed it right into the man's cheek. The reaction was quick. The man, frightened by the aggressive nun, and realizing (without understanding her English) that she meant business, quickly took off the watch and gave it to her.

Meanwhile, the bus had come to a stop and this gave the sister the opportunity to get off immediately. She had become so nervous that her only desire was to get home. When she returned to her friend's house with her watch still tightly grasped in her hand, her friend said: "But how, in heaven's name, did this man ever get into your purse?" "I don't know," was the puzzled answer.

Then the sister opened her purse and found her watch tucked safely between her notebooks and papers. In total consternation, she cried out: "My God, now I have two watches—and one of them I stole!" Her hypervigilance had turned her into a robber.

Sometimes we may be more frightened of people than we need to be. Maybe on her next trip to the market, the sister should wear a watch on each arm so that at least one will be stolen.

Thursday, January 28

If anything has affected me deeply since I have been living in Pamplona Alta, it has been the children. I have realized that since my eighteenth year I have not been around children. The seminary, the university, and all the teaching positions that followed were the worlds of young adults, worlds in which children and old people hardly entered. Yet here I am surrounded by boys and girls running up to me, giving me kisses, climbing up to my shoulders, throwing balls at me, and constantly asking for some sign of interest in their lives.

The children always challenge me to live in the present. They want me to be with them here and now, and they find it hard to understand that I might have other things to do or to think about. After all my experiences with psychotherapy, I suddenly have discovered the great healing power of children. Every time Pablito, Johnny, and Maria run up to welcome me, pick up my suitcase, and bring me to my "roof-room," I marvel at their ability to be fully present to me. Their uninhibited expression of affection and their willingness to receive it pull me directly into the moment and invite me to celebrate life where it is found. Whereas in the past coming home meant time to study, to write letters, and to prepare for classes, it now first of all means time to play.

In the beginning, I had to get used to finding a little boy under my bed, a little girl in my closet, and a teenager under my table, but now I am disappointed when I find my friends asleep at night. I did not know what to expect when I came to Pamplona Alta. I wondered how the poverty, the lack of good food and good housing would affect me; I was afraid of becoming depressed by the misery I would see. But God showed me something else first: affectionate, open, and playful children who are telling me about love and life in ways no book was ever able to do. I now realize that only when I can enter with the children into their joy will I be able to enter also with them into their poverty and pain. God obviously wants me to walk into the world of suffering with a little child on each hand.

Friday, January 29

Charles, Tom, Pete, Sister Marge, and I went to the beach today. Charles explained: "When there are five Fridays in a month, we cancel our team meeting on the fifth Friday and go to the beach to swim and to have a good meal." We drove to Punta Hermosa, about a half-hour north of Lima. Huge waves came rolling up to the beach in rapid succession. Compared with the waves of the Atlantic Ocean, these waves were immense. It was great fun to try to "catch a wave" at the right time and to be carried in on its crest. I failed most of the time, and often found myself spinning under a wall of water, wondering where I would emerge. I found that not only the children but the waves of the Pacific have healing power! They wash away my preoccupations and make me smile in grati-

tude to him who led his people through the Red Sea and the Jordan
and calmed the storms on the lake.

Saturday, January 30

Dust is probably my greatest physical problem here. Wherever
I turn, I encounter dust. Walking on the sandy street, I am always
surrounded by small clouds of dust, and when a car passes the dust
becomes like a heavy fog that vanishes only slowly. Everything in
my room is covered with a layer of fine dust. When I want to write
a letter, I first blow the dust away; when I want to drink tea, I have
first to wash the dust off the cup; and when I want to go to sleep,
I have first to shake the dust from the covers and the sheets. It
settles in my hair, ears, and nose. It crawls into my socks, shirts,
and pants; and it creeps in between the pages of the books I am
reading. Since it is quite humid here, the dust sticks easily to
whatever it lands on. This gives me a nearly permanent desire for
a shower. Only the realization that the pleasure of feeling clean
would probably not last longer than five minutes has helped me
to develop a certain indifference to this dustbowl.

For the many people who like to keep their houses, their bodies,
and their small children clean and fresh-looking, dust remains a
resolute enemy. The only hope is that the water pipeline that has
recently been built to Pamplona Alta will enable trees, plants, and
grass to grow fast enough so that within a decade its people will
win the war against the dust.

Sunday, January 31

The Gospel of this Sunday touches a sensitive nerve in me. It
speaks about the authority with which Jesus speaks, heals, and
exorcises demons. People who saw Jesus said: "What is this? A
new teaching, taught with authority!" When Jesus addressed the
people, his words had healing power and even were able to make
evil spirits obey.

All of this stands in contrast to my own experience in preaching
here. I wonder if anyone is really listening, and I often experience
my words as totally powerless. This morning, while I was trying
to say a few things with conviction, I found myself face to face
with a man who was sound asleep. He was sitting in the corner
of the first pew and kept reminding me, in his passive state, that
my words had absolutely no authority for him.

The most important question for me is not, "How do I touch people?" but, "How do I live the word I am speaking?" In Jesus, no division existed between his words and his actions, between what he said and what he did. Jesus' words were his action, his words were events. They not only spoke about changes, cures, new life, but they actually created them. In this sense, Jesus is truly the Word made flesh; in that Word all is created and by that Word all is recreated.

Saintliness means living without division between word and action. If I would truly live in my own life the word I am speaking, my spoken words would become actions, and miracles would happen whenever I opened my mouth. The Gospel of today thus confronts me not so much with a question about pastoral tactics or strategy, but with an invitation to deep personal conversion.

5.

An Inner and Outer Struggle

Monday, February 1

The nights in Pamplona Alta are filled with loud sounds. Until late at night, music from different parties pours through the many holes in my little room. Around 2:00 A.M., buses come to the neighborhood to pick up the merchants to take them to the warehouses where they buy the products which they will sell later in the day in the market. Since the people are afraid to wait outside of their houses with money in their pockets, the bus drivers blow their horns loudly to tell the people of their arrival. From 2:00 to 3:00 A.M., these loud sounds of the dilapidated buses fill the air. Shortly after 4:00 A.M., the roosters start their calls; and by 6:00 A.M. the bread-carrying boy blows his whistles to sell his fresh-baked loaves. Strangely enough, it is quite peaceful between 6:00 and 8:00 A.M. But then the huge loudspeaker of a neighboring school blasts the national anthem over the roofs and makes everyone part of the first instructions to the children.

Parties, buses, roosters, breadboys, and loudspeakers keep the sounds floating through the night and the early morning. During my first weeks here, I thought I would never get used to it; but now these sounds have become a familiar background noise that no longer interrupts my sleep, my prayers, or my reading, but simply reminds me in my roof-room that I am in the middle of a world of people who have to struggle not only hard, but also loudly in order to survive.

Tuesday, February 2

Today we celebrate the presentation of our Lord in the temple. I have been thinking about this mysterious event. Mary and Joseph took Jesus to Jerusalem "to present him to the Lord" and to offer the Lord the sacrifice of the poor, "a pair of turtledoves or two young pigeons." There in the temple they met two old people, Simeon and Anna, who sensed the sacredness of the moment and spoke words about the child that astounded his parents.

Every time I try to meditate on a sacred event such as this, I find myself tempted to think about it in an intellectual way. But today I realized more strongly than ever before that I simply have to be there. I have to travel with Mary and Joseph to Jerusalem, walk with them on the busy temple square, join the thousands of simple people in offering their simple gifts, feel somewhat lost and awed by it all, and listen to two unknown old people who have something to say, something that sounds very strange and even frightening. Why do I want more? Why do I want to add a comment to it all? It is as if I want to keep some distance. But the story is so simple, so crystal clear, so unpretentious. I do not have to do anything with it. I do not have to explain or examine these events. I simply have to step into them and allow them to surround me, to leave me silent. I do not have to master or capture them. I have only to be carried by them to places where I am as small, quiet, and inconspicuous as the child of Mary and Joseph.

Something of that happened to me as I went through the day. I kept seeing Simeon and Anna; and instead of disregarding them as two pious old church mice who disturbed me with their aggressive predictions, I sat down for a while and allowed them to speak and me to listen. I heard Simeon and Anna many times over during the day, and I suddenly realized that they have been trying to speak to me for a long time.

Wednesday, February 3

Writing letters has become extremely important for me during this long absence from home. I have discovered in myself a growing freedom to express to my friends my feelings simply and directly. A deep change is taking place in me as I write down what is most joyful and most painful for me. I find myself hardly interested in telling about the daily events of my outer life, but strongly compelled to share openly, even nakedly, what is happening within me. I no longer feel that I have anything to lose: all I have I can give. Writing letters is becoming a way of self-emptying, of being nothing more and nothing less than someone who wants to give and receive love. It seems that the poor people of Pamplona Alta have taught me this. They keep telling me without words: "All you have is yourself, so do not hide it from those you love."

Thursday, February 4

When I first came to Lima, Bill McCarthy invited me to visit his home in Andahuaylas. I met Bill for the first time a few years ago at Yale, when he spent a sabbatical year there. Bill McCarthy is a Maryknoller who spent most of his professional life teaching church history at the Maryknoll seminary in New York state. Although he entered the Maryknoll society to become a missioner, he found himself for many years teaching future missioners at home. But after his sabbatical at Yale, Bill asked to be sent to the missions. He went to Cochabamba for language training and after that joined Joe, a young Maryknoller, to start a new mission in Andahuaylas, a seven-year-old *barrio* in eastern Lima.

Today I saw Bill's new home and got some impressions of the neighborhood and the pastoral work Bill and Joe are developing. Ten years ago, Andahuaylas was still a large hacienda at the outskirts of Lima. Now it is a *pueblo joven* (young town) with hundreds of small houses under construction. It looks very much like Pamplona Alta but as yet has neither running water nor electricity. Most of the people try to earn their living as *ambulantes,* walking vendors in the market place.

Bill and Joe, with the help of Lucho, the catechist, are trying to develop small Christian "base" communities. They go around visiting people in their homes and encouraging them to meet regularly with people from their block, discussing common problems in the light of the Gospel, studying the Scriptures, and praying.

"How do you motivate people to form such a community?" I asked. Bill answered: "Well, we first explain to people that the Church started in the homes of people and not in church buildings. We read from the Acts of the Apostles and suggest that just as the apostles built the Church in the first century in the Middle East, so we can build the Church now, in the twentieth century."

It was an effort that required much patience and perseverance. "It is very slow work," Bill said. "The people who live here work long hours and when they come home from the market, they often are so tired that they do not have the energy to have meetings and to study and pray. On their few free days, they like to rest and play soccer. It is important for us to understand their condition." In addition to the different basic communities, which were slowly developing, Bill, Joe, and Lucho also started two liturgical centers for the Sunday Eucharist. One was in the chapel of the former owner of the hacienda, and the other was in an open lot that was set aside for the future church. Attendance was low: thirty people at one place, ten at the other. "We are just beginning," Bill said, "and we are still groping for the right way to be pastors here."

This short visit created in me a desire to learn how to build a church from the ground up, to let the people themselves give shape and form to their own Christian life. This approach is far from the old triumphalism of the gold-decorated churches in downtown Lima, far from the church of great visibility and power. A very humble and inconspicuous church builds upon the rock of faith, hope, and love.

Friday, February 5

Unexpectedly, I am experiencing a deep depression. Perhaps the days of friendly greetings and introductions have kept me on an artificial level of contentment that prevented me from acknowledging my deep-seated feeling of uselessness. The depression seems to hit me from all sides at once. I have very little strength to deal with it. The most pervasive feeling is that of being an outsider, someone who doesn't have a home, who is tolerated by his surroundings but not accepted, liked but not loved. I experience myself as a stuttering, superfluous presence and the people around me as indifferent, distant, cold, uninterested, and at times hostile. The men, women, and children I see on the streets seem to be so far from me that I despair when I think of them as people to whom I am sent. I crave personal attention and affection. The life in a parish suddenly strikes me as cool, mechanical, and routine. I cannot find a person with whom I can go beyond asking informative questions. I desire friendships, a moment of personal attention, a little interest in my individual experiences. The world around me appears to me as a complex pattern of words, actions, and responses in which I am caught, an entrapping net of baptisms, weddings, masses, and meetings. Meanwhile, I keep hearing: "This is the way we do things here. You should just try to become part of it. If you have problems, just stay with it and you will find out that our ways are the best."

The fact that my feelings are so general and touch practically everything I see, hear, or do, shows that I am dealing with a genuine depression and not with critical observations. I have little control over it. It feels like a form of possession. I try to pray for deliverance, but prayer does not bring any relief. It even appears dark and frightening. What else can I do but wait?

Saturday, February 6

The emotions of loneliness, isolation, and separation are as strong today as they were yesterday. It seems as if the depression has not lost any of its intensity. In fact, it has become worse. My mind keeps asking: "Why does nobody show me any personal attention?" My sensation that my feelings, experiences, history, and character are irrelevant to the people I meet, and that I am primarily used as a body that can take over routine functions, keeps ripping me apart from the inside. What I am craving is not so much recognition, praise, or admiration, as simple friendship. There may be some around me, but I cannot perceive or receive it. Within me lies a deadness that leaves me cold, tired, and rigid.

I attended a small workshop given by Pete Ruggere and Tom Burns about the basic meaning of being a Christian, but little of what was said reached my heart. I realized that the only thing I really wanted was a handshake, an embrace, a kiss, or a smile; I received none. Finally, I fell asleep in the late afternoon to escape it all.

Sunday, February 7

In times of depression, one of the few things to hold onto is a schedule. When there is little inner vitality, the outer order of the day allows me to continue to function somewhat coherently. It is like a scaffolding put around a building that needs restoration.

I got up at 6:30 A.M. and assisted Charles in the 7:00 o'clock Mass. At 9:00 A.M. I celebrated Mass myself and gave a sermon. From 10:30 to 12:30, I wrote a few letters. After lunch, at 2:00 P.M., Tom took me to a little fund-raising fiesta in Los Angeles, one of the sections of Pamplona Alta. The small Christian community there wants to build a chapel and decided to have a mini-fiesta on one of the street corners. They had games to play and food to buy. I picked up Pablito, Johnny, Maria, and her little girlfriend so they could try out the food and the games. They had a good time.

At 7:00 P.M. I was back at the parish and attended a short meeting in which two couples who had just finished a marriage encounter were welcomed home by other couples. Around 9:00 Charles, Tom, Pete, Larry, Patricia, a visiting Mercy Sister, and I went out to have a pizza. At 11:00 I was back home. I prayed my evening prayers and went to bed. The events of this "uneventful" day kept me mentally alive. I feel I am simply waiting for the day and the hour that the cloud of depression will pass by and I can see the sun again.

Monday, February 8

Today a two-week summer course in theological reflection began in downtown Lima. It is the twelfth time that this course, inspired and directed by Gustavo Gutiérrez, has been held. It is one of the most significant yearly events in the church in Lima. This year, three thousand "pastoral agents" are participating. People come not only from all the districts of Peru, but also from Chile, Brazil, Colombia, Ecuador, Paraguay, Uruguay, Argentina, Panama, and Nicaragua. It is a young, vital, and enthusiastic student body.

The summer course has three levels. The first level is an introductory theology course. The second and third levels have different emphases each year. This year, the second-level course deals with Christology and the third-level course with Spirituality.

I decided to take the course on Spirituality. From 3:00 to 5:00 P.M. there are discussion groups, and from 5:30 to 8:00 P.M. lectures. Gustavo Gutiérrez gave the first two lectures tonight. He discussed Christian spirituality under three headings: (1) living according to the Spirit; (2) the encounter with Christ; and (3) a global way of life.

Gustavo is a lively teacher. Holding a microphone in one hand and gesturing vigorously with the other, he takes his audience through theological hills and valleys and shows one fascinating panorama after the other. Impatiently, he shuffles his papers and complains that he cannot say it all in a few hours. He gives the impression of a man who has an enormous treasure to share and is continually frustrated that he cannot show his gifts all at once. But in a short time he is able to give his listeners a desire for theological understanding, offer them challenging perspectives, and make them aware of the privilege of being a Christian today. One of the points that stuck with me was his view on the interior life. The interior life, Gustavo said, does not refer to the psychological reality that one reaches through introspection, but is the life lived free from the constraining power of the law in the Pauline sense. It is a life free to love. Thus the spiritual life is the place of true freedom. When we are able to throw off the compulsions and coercions that come from outside of us and can allow the Holy Spirit, God's love, to be our only guide, then we can live a truly free, interior, and spiritual life.

Tuesday, February 9

Gustavo's lecture today was entitled "The Journey of a People in Search of God." It was a brilliant treatment of a spirituality of leaving, walking, and entering: the people of God are called to leave their situation of slavery and walk through the desert in order to enter the land of freedom, where they can own the land and live in justice and peace.

In the light of many biblical texts, Gustavo explored the meaning of this journey of freedom. His main assertion was that the search for God *is* the search for freedom, and that the search for freedom *is* the search for God. Many people who are deeply involved in the struggle for water, for light, for schools, and for health care do not perceive this as a search for God. And many who attend churches, walk in processions, and bless their houses with holy water do not experience this as part of a struggle for freedom. This is not uncommon. Even the Hebrews who left Egypt did not fully understand the meaning of the events in which they were participating. It is precisely in the reflection on the events of the people that the search for God and the struggle for liberty are connected and can deepen each other.

Of particular importance to me was Gustavo's notion that the journey of the people is not a journey from nothing to something, but from something to something. When we speak about a movement from slavery to freedom, from scarcity to possession, and from exploitation to justice, we should not think and act as if freedom, possession, and justice are only on one end of the polarities. In fact, in Egypt there existed freedom, possessions, and justice. That is why at times the Hebrews wanted to return to Egypt, and that too is the reason why a desire for full freedom, possession, and justice could grow. You can only desire what you already know or have in some measure.

This, therefore, also means that the search for God is a search for him whom we have already met, and who has already shown us his mercy and love. The desire for God makes us aware that we already know him.

For me, these thoughts are important because they point to a ministry that first of all recognizes the gifts of God that are already present. It is by acknowledging these gifts and lifting them up as signs of God's presence in our midst that we can start leaving, walking, and entering. The journey is not a journey of despairing people who have never seen God nor tasted freedom; rather, it is a journey of hopeful people, who know that God is with them and will lead them to a freedom of which they have already tasted the first fruits.

Wednesday, February 10

I continue to be impressed by the thousands of people who are actively participating in the summer course. They are not only people from all parts of Latin America, but also from very different stages and walks of life. There are quite a few priests and sisters, mostly Americans, British, and Irish; but the majority of this assembly is made up of people who have been born and raised in the poor *barrios* and have become active pastoral agents in the process of liberation. They know their own people and they have learned to think with one eye on the Gospel and one eye on the plight of their compatriots. In the Latin American Church, the people themselves are showing the direction in which to go. They are open and hospitable to strangers who want to participate, but the struggle is theirs and they themselves provide the leadership.

Many of these people are very young. They work in their different districts as catechists, social workers, project coordinators, and so on. All of them are steeped in the Bible; with it they live and struggle. They have come to think of themselves as the people of God called to the promised land. They all know it will be a long, arduous, and often painful journey; but they also know that no worldly powers can make them give up their struggle and return to the state of submission and resignation from which they came.

In his lecture today, Manuel Diaz Mateos, S.J., developed a spirituality of the marginal person and the stranger. He pointed to Abel (the weak one), Noah, Job, Ruth, the innocent children, the widows, the publicans, and the Samaritans as proof of God's special love and attention for those who live on the periphery of society and who are considered weak. For me, this presentation opened up a vision of ministry that I keep losing, although I am constantly called back to it. It is the vision that ministry means first of all searching for God where people are lost, confused, broken, and poor. Often I have gone to such people to bring them back to God, to the sacraments, and to the church. But that is acting and living as if God is where I am, and as if my first task is to bring others to my place. When, however, God is with the poor and marginal, then I have to dare to go there, live there, and find him there. I now realize that I can be with people without having to make them think my thoughts and say my words. I can be free to listen and slowly to discern where God shows his merciful face to me.

Thursday, February 11

Every day of the summer course, the students meet for two hours in "commissions," discussion groups in which the lectures of the previous day are discussed and appropriated. I am a member of a discussion group with twenty participants. We are a very interesting little community. The majority are Peruvians, but there are two Chileans, a Uruguayan, a Nicaraguan, a Swiss, and myself. All of these people are active in some form of pastoral care, and most of them are leaders in their own communities.

The discussions are extremely poignant, with little abstract thinking going on. People constantly test the ideas presented in the lectures against their own daily experiences and try to let these experiences be their source of ongoing theological reflections. Some of these experiences are harsh. They are experiences of harassment, exploitation, imprisonment, and torture. Everyone is aware that the road to liberation is rough and uncharted, asking for a commitment that goes as far as the willingness to sacrifice one's life. It is overwhelming for me to hear these young men and women speak so directly and articulately about their love for Jesus Christ, their desire to give everything to the realization of his Kingdom, their willingness to be and remain poor with the poor, and their joy to be chosen for this great task of liberation. There is little sentimentality and little piety. The word that dominates all the discussions is *la lucha,* the struggle.

Today the main topic was prayer. Within a few minutes, the growing charismatic movement (Neo-Pentecostalism) became the main subject. Most participants considered the charismatic movement as appealing primarily to the middle- and upper-class youth; as offering a spiritual experience without social consequences; as closely linked to other conservative organizations such as the *cursillistas,* as a spiritual weapon in the hands of the oppressing classes. People didn't hesitate to say that prayer, as seen and practiced in many charismatic groups, was not Christian prayer since it does not come from nor lead to the *lucha* for the liberation of God's people.

Reflecting on this discussion, I feel quite uncomfortable. The sweeping generalizations about the charismatic movement seem to deny the need of many people to find a still point in their lives where they can listen to the voice of God in the midst of a sad and war-ridden world. This desire for inner tranquility and the direct experience of God's Spirit can become a form of escape from the struggle for liberation, but it does not have to be that way.

During my one-semester stay in Rome, I participated actively in a charismatic prayer group at the Gregorian University. In many ways it kept me spiritually alive during that time. I never experienced this prayer group as an escape mechanism, but as a source of spiritual revitalization that freed me from many fears and compulsions and allowed me to dedicate myself more generously to the service of others.

I even have the feeling that those who want to be active in the struggle for freedom for a lifetime will need an increasingly strong and personal experience of the presence of the Spirit of God in their lives. I would not be surprised if, within a few years, a search for new disciplines of prayer were to occupy the minds of many Christians who struggle with the poor for liberation. I hope that the division between the charismatic movement and the liberation movement will not grow so wide that it creates a *lucha* within the Christian community.

Friday, February 12

The lectures given yesterday and today were disappointing; they consisted of many words but few connections with daily experiences. One speaker spoke eloquently about compassion as the most important attribute of Jesus, and another talked about the centrality of contemplation in the history of Christian spirituality. Each covered a huge area of Christian thought, but neither was able to touch his audience. It was sad to see how everyone had a hard time staying awake during lectures on such life-giving realities as compassion and contemplation.

The discussion group showed a lot more vitality. We were asked to list core traits of a Latin American spirituality. Fifteen aspects of Christian spirituality were written on the blackboard and everyone was asked to choose three that were most important for Latin America today. Everyone agreed that "compassion" had too many passive connotations. Some argued that, in a world in which the largest part of the population is oppressed and exploited, the word compassion sounds too personalistic and suggests a sentimental acceptance of the status quo. However, when people started to choose the three most important traits, many still considered compassion an essential quality in the struggle for liberation. After much discussion, we came to the conclusion that every Christian is called to a radical commitment to establish the Kingdom of God on earth, and that for the Latin American Christian this means a compassionate struggle to liberate the poor. Everyone stressed that this formulation was inadequate and did not cover the whole of a Christian spirituality for Latin America, but nobody denied that this formulation captured the main thrust of the "New Church."

I was struck by the repeated use of the word *lucha*. This word is used to counteract a passive and fatalistic stance towards the misery of the masses and to stress the urgency of an active—even aggressive—involvement in the war against poverty, oppression, and exploitation. However, I tried to locate a concrete idea of this *lucha* in the daily life of the Christian community, and of the Christian strategy of this struggle. In the absence of such a concrete idea and strategy, there is a danger that the struggle for the full liberation of the people will be narrowed down to a "fight for rights." This type of *lucha* can easily lead to a fanaticism no longer guided by the joy and peace of God's Kingdom, but by a human instinct seeking to replace one form of oppression with another.

Saturday, February 13

Over the week, my depression has worn off a bit. It has not been lifted or healed, but it has lost its most painful edges in the midst of the summer course. I was helped by the insight that I had to move directly and aggressively in the direction I want to go. Waiting to be shown the best people to meet, the best places to visit, the best events to become part of, only feeds my depression. I am sure that I will find my direction in life when I search actively, move around with open eyes and ears, ask questions, and—in the midst of all that—pray constantly to discover God's will. The Lord searches for me, I am sure, but only when I search for him too will I encounter him and will his word for me become clear. Every time I slip into another depression, I notice that I have given up the struggle to find God and have fallen back into an attitude of spiteful waiting.

Sunday, February 14

In Peru, people celebrate Carnival by throwing water at each other. Innocent passersby are often surprised by a shower, and buses and cars with open windows make attractive targets for water-throwers. A few years ago, this was causing so many accidents that the government decided that the only Carnival days were the four Sundays of February, disregarding the date of Ash Wednesday.

My friends had instructed me to wear old clothes on these wet Sundays. Wherever I went today I saw little groups of teenagers on the street corners ready to attack any dry person with anything that can hold water: balloons, pots and pans, and even large buckets. I also noticed eager water-throwers perched on the roofs to surprise people entering and leaving the buildings. Some people simply decide to stay home during Carnival. One of the parish choirs decided not to sing today, because they don't like to sing in church while soaking wet.

I took a bus to Las Flores, a large *barrio* on the southern outskirts of Lima, to visit a community of English Benedictines. Unlike many other buses I had ridden on here, there were few broken windows on this bus, but at every stop people getting on or off were thoroughly drenched. Everyone seemed to enjoy the game, although even well-dressed people looked like drowned cats as they stepped on the bus. The driver tried to escape the water-throwing youths by stopping between official stops to let people off and by letting people on at any place they raised their hands. He played the game with a good spirit. He lost a few and won a few.

Most people, from very young to very old, take it all with good-natured laughter. "As long as they don't put paint in the water," a woman said to me, "it's a lot of fun. It is so hot here anyhow that you are dry again before you are home." I made it to the monks moist but not wet.

Monday, February 15

During the last few years, I have received several letters from Marist Sister Teresa asking for money to help some Peruvian ex-prisoners. Today Sister Teresa took me to Lurigancho, the huge prison where she works. It is hard to describe what I saw, heard, and smelled during my four hours in Lurigancho. I want to record at least some of my impressions.

Lurigancho is a world within a world. About four thousand men live inside a small area surrounded by huge walls and watchtowers. They are there for reasons varying from murder to buying cocaine on the street. The majority of these men have never been sentenced and have no idea when their case will come to court or how long they will have to stay behind those walls. Some have been there for a few months, others for more than seven years; some are there for the first time, others old regulars for whom Lurigancho has become a second home. Some seem friendly and gentle, others silent and menacing.

Lurigancho impressed me as a microcosm of the extremes in life. Within the prison I visited several small libraries with helpful librarians. Everywhere were men weaving baskets, playing ball, sleeping in the sun, and standing on corners talking together. Less visible but no less real are the knives, guns, and drugs hidden in the corners, closets, and cells. What do these men do? For most of them there is no work, no way to keep busy except weaving baskets. Yet much activity goes on. Gangs fight each other, prisoners kill each other, groups pray together, men study together. There are meek, quiet, and unassuming people; there are also aggressive and dangerous men who are feared, avoided, or kept under control.

What struck me first was the enormous chaos. Once we had made our way through the gates, it seemed that all discipline was gone. Since most of the thirteen huge cellblocks were open, we could walk freely in, out, and through. Prisoners were walking around with little restriction and behaved as if they were in charge. Most of them were naked from the waist up; many just wore swimming trunks. Some showed big scars on their bodies, the result of self-inflicted cuts that had put them in the hospital and allowed them to escape from torture. The food consists of bread in the morning, rice and beans in the afternoon, and soup in the evening. It is brought in huge containers and put on the patio of the cellblock for anyone who wants it. But many feed themselves in other ways. They get money from their visitors and buy food from the different black market stores or bars.

There is as much horror, cruelty, and violence as there is friendliness, human play, and simple village life. One of the most surprising things to me was that all the prisoners can receive visitors two times a week. During visiting days the population practically doubles. Women come with large baskets of food, some to bring it to their imprisoned relatives, others to sell it to those who have money. One cellblock looked like a lively market place. There were different food stands, and all over the place groups of people were sitting on the floor, talking or playing cards. It was not all that different from the marketplace in Ciudad de Dios.

Prisoners can take their wives or girlfriends to their cells with them. Cellmates simply stay away for a few hours, and when one of them has a visitor the favor is returned. Most prisoners live together according to the area of town or the district they come from. The nature of their crime seems to have little to do with the company they keep; first offenders often live together with experienced killers.

Often cellblocks fight with each other. Walls get broken down, windows smashed, and when there is enough alcohol around, people get wounded or killed. Once in a while things get so far out of hand that the *guardia republicana,* the police force, moves in. On February 2 the police carried out a wild and indiscriminately brutal assault on one cellblock. Tear gas was used and random shooting took place. During the four-hour rampage prisoners were severely beaten, tortured, and wounded. When it was all over, three men were dead.

While talking about all this, one of the prisoners brought me to a little flower garden he had carefully cultivated. Proudly he showed me the lovely roses that had just come out. It was hard for me to put it all together. But that is Lurigancho.

On our walk, we passed a pavilion that we could not enter. "That is where the homosexuals live together," one of my prisoner-guides told me. I saw a lot of prisoners hanging around the building and gazing through the fence into the open lot. I suddenly felt as though I were at a zoo. One prisoner said: "Look, those are the gays." It was clear to me that they were really talking about transvestites. There is a lot of sex between men in Lurigancho, but in this section lived the real "queens," who had asked to be together to have some degree of freedom from harassment. They were locked up by their own wish more than by that of any prison authority. I have never seen humans look at caged people in such a way. It made me feel something very dark and evil.

Finally, Teresa led me to the pavilion of the foreigners. It was located at some distance from the other cellblocks we had just seen. When we went in, I had the strange sensation of walking into an exclusive country club. On the open patio, blond young men in tiny swimming suits were playing racketball or sunbathing on a towel. Their tanned and well-fed bodies were a stark contrast to the dark, scarred bodies of the poor Peruvians I had just visited. These were prosperous, middle-class Europeans, Americans, or Australians who came from a world light-years away from the dark, dirty cells of the other pavilions. A minute after I entered, I met a young Dutchman who was glad to meet a fellow countryman and to speak his mother tongue. He gave me the grand tour. The main living space consisted of a huge, open hall where people spent most of their time. The atmosphere was that of an exposition hall. In the center stood workbenches where people could do a little carpentry. Scattered about were stands where food and drinks were sold, and all over the place people were playing cards, chess, and checkers. The place looked clean and well-kept—more like an amusement park than a prison. My Dutch guide showed me his bedroom. It was a small wooden room with two bunkbeds. "I paid $200 for it," the Dutchman explained. "You can get anything here when you pay for it." He introduced me to his roommate, a tall, good-looking American from Washington, D.C. "It doesn't look too bad here," I said. "Oh no," they responded. "In fact it's quite all right here, except that you're locked up and don't know for how long."

I soon found out that they both were arrested because of drugs. "I sold some drugs to an undercover policeman, and that got me here," the Dutchman said. As he and his American friend talked more, I got the picture. Since they had been arrested on drug charges, they now have to buy their way out, and legal help is extremely expensive. Every step of the way can cost a fortune. But money came from Holland or the United States through the embassies. The American was lucky to have his wife in Lima, who could visit two times a week and bring in all the food they wanted. "We don't touch the prison food," the Dutchman said. "My American friend's wife brings us steaks and good soup, and we make our own meals." I asked how they spend their time. "We read a lot and play games, talk and sit in the sun," they said. "And here we can get any drugs we want."

I had never expected this strange island of decadence in the center of the Lurigancho prison. If I ever saw discrimination, it was here. The poor lived in miserable poverty, the wealthy built their own country club, and these two worlds lived side by side behind the prison walls.

But this living side by side was not as simple as it might seem. At night the foreigners had to protect their domain against attacks from the poor pavilions. My hosts explained: "We had to organize our own guard to keep the others from our roof and to prevent them from breaking in and stealing our stuff."

When we were let out through the heavy gates and stepped onto the bus to go home, I knew that only a very simple, pure, and holy person would be able to work with these men for any length of time. Just being there for four hours had made me see that Teresa must be such a person. She moved in this world without fear, open, practical, unsentimental, and with a deep sense of God's love. She saw it all clearly, but was not entangled in it. The men knew that she was one of the few who had no second motives. She was just there to be of help and that was all. Surrounded by the complexity of the dark world, the simple love of God can easily be discerned.

Tuesday, February 16

Today I went to the airport to pick up some galley proofs that were sent to me by my publisher through one of the airlines. Naively, I thought that it would be a matter of a few minutes. But when I got to the cargo area I received some papers to take to a network of offices, officials, cash registers, and desks that was more complex than I have experienced before in my life. Every time I had made it through one hoop, another awaited me. A sea of people, as nervous and confused as I, added to the endless waiting. Meanwhile, young boys offered to do it all for me for some money, trying to convince me that they knew the right way to the package. However, I clung to my growing stack of documents with the anxiety of a man whose life is in danger. Finally, after three hours, I made it to the warehouse where I could see the package. An hour later, a man from customs came with some more documents and let me open the package and identify the galleys. For a moment I thought that now I could take them home with me, but I soon found out that I was only halfway through the process. Two more payments had to be made, and at least three more offices with long waiting lines had to be visited. At that time, I gave in to the boys and gave them the money to do the work for me. They took my papers and gave me their I.D., and I left the airport with their promise that tomorrow morning I would get my package.

David Ritter, a Jefferson City, Missouri, priest who has worked in Peru for three years and who drove me to the airport for this "quick errand," prevented me from going crazy in the midst of it all. He smiled and laughed about it and explained how this way of doing things gave work and money to many Peruvians, and gave me a chance to practice my patience.

I am amazed how hard it is to just take things the Peruvian way, use my time to talk with people, practice my Spanish, and simply flow with the stream. After all, I might profit more from waiting than from being waited on. My frustration, anger, anxiety, and impatience, however, clearly showed me how far I truly am from enjoying solidarity with the poor!

Wednesday, February 17

After two more hours of running from office to office, talking to an endless succession of people, and paying more tips, I finally got my package. Then I returned to the course on spirituality and listened to Gustavo Gutiérrez's lecture on the "traits of a contemporary spirituality in Latin America." It was the most impressive presentation of the course so far, and it brought together many of the themes that have occupied our minds during the last ten days.

Gustavo stressed the "eruption of the poor into the history of Latin America." The suffering poor have become the pastoral agents who point to a new way of being Christian, a new spirituality, characterized by a call to conversion not only of individual people, but of the church as a whole. This conversion promises a way of living in which effectiveness is sought in a climate of grace. Such a climate allows us to experience a real joy that comes forth from suffering, helps us to live as "spiritual infants" with the poor while fighting against poverty, and makes it possible to find freedom in a communal life. Although all of these are among the classical themes of a Christian spirituality, they have found new articulation and meaning in the context of the eruption of the poor.

What struck me most was Gustavo's ability to integrate a

spirituality of struggle for freedom with a spirituality of personal growth. He placed great emphasis on the importance of personal friendship, affective relationships, "useless" prayer, and intimate joy as essential elements of a true struggle for liberation.

The method Gustavo used was of special interest to me. As the source for his spirituality, he used documents that came forth from the suffering church in Latin America. A text written by a Christian community in Lima, declarations by the bishops of Guatemala and Chile, sermons of Bishop Romero of El Salvador, letters by Rutilio Grande, Nestor Paz, and Louis Espinal, and statements by the mothers of the "vanished ones" all formed the sources from which Gustavo developed a spirituality for Latin America. It was a powerful example of reflection on the suffering experienced in persecution and martyrdom. I was not surprised, therefore, with the warm and enthusiastic reception that Gustavo's vision met. He is a genuine theologian, a man who breaks the bread of God's word for thousands of people and offers hope, courage, and confidence.

Thursday, February 18

What does it mean to live a religious life in Latin America? During the last months I have often asked myself: Would it be possible to live with a small group of dedicated people in the midst of a *pueblo joven* and practice there the disciplines of prayer and meditation in such a way that the group would become a center of hope for the neighborhood?

What I see now are many dedicated and generous people involved in different projects. They are very busy, distracted, pressured, and restless, and often very tired. They hardly have time and space for each other, let alone for spiritual reading, theological reflection, sharing of religious experiences, mental prayer, the liturgy of the hours, or any other religious practice.

But how would it be if, in the midst of the very poor, a small group of men and women created a space for people to celebrate God's presence? How would it be if, instead of running in all directions, these men and women could draw others into prayer, silence, reflection, sharing of experiences, and singing God's praise? Maybe it is just a romantic dream, but it is a dream that continues to press itself on me.

This was the last day of the summer course. At seven-thirty, Bishop Herman Schmidt celebrated a festive liturgy with the three thousand students and teachers of the course. There was a general mood of gratitude. All the people I spoke with communicated a real excitement about having been part of this event and a desire to go back to work and share with others the new insights and experiences that the course had offered.

Among the hundreds of ideas that passed through my mind in the past days, one in particular has stayed with me. It is the simple thought that true theological reflection can convert a paralyzing experience into an experience of hope. That seemed to me what this course had done for many. Most of the students work with the poor, often in depressing, discouraging, and even agonizing circumstances. The reflections of the course gave us a consciousness of a divine and liberating presence in the midst of it all and freed us from fatalism and despair. We came to experience that agony really means struggle, and that God is in that struggle with us. And so a new joy could grow, and we could become aware that it is a privilege to work with the poor and suffer with them for a new world.

Thus the final liturgy could be a genuine celebration, a lifting up of God's presence among us and among the poor, and an expression of gratitude for what we had seen with our own eyes, heard with our own ears, and touched with our own hands (1 John 1:1).

Gratitude is one of the most visible characteristics of the poor I have come to know. I am always surrounded by words of thanks: "thanks for your visit, your blessing, your sermon, your prayer, your gifts, your presence with us." Even the smallest and most necessary goods are a reason for gratitude. This all-pervading gratitude is the basis for celebration. Not only are the poor grateful for life, but they also celebrate life constantly. A visit, a reunion, a simple meeting are always like little celebrations. Every time a new gift is recognized, there are songs or toasts, words of congratulation, or something to eat and drink. And every gift is shared. "Have a drink, take some fruit, eat our bread" is the response to every visit I make, and this is what I see people do for each other. All of life is a gift, a gift to be celebrated, a gift to be shared.

Thus the poor are a eucharistic people, people who know to say thanks to God, to life, to each other. They may not come to Mass, they may not participate in many church celebrations. But in their hearts they are deeply religious, because for them all of life is a long fiesta with God.

Sunday, February 21

After more than a month in Pamplona Alta, I have come to believe strongly that a "pastoral presence" is more important than any plan or project. This conviction has grown out of the observation that, more than anything else, people want you to share their lives. This afternoon I simply walked to where I heard music. About six blocks from where I live, I soon saw people dancing around a tree and cutting it down bit by bit. It proved to be a carnival celebration that is popular in the jungle of Peru, and that some emigrants had transported to Pamplona Alta.

Although nobody knew me, it didn't take long for people to offer me a drink and to make me part of their fiesta. One member of the band told me without blinking an eye that he was a drug dealer and had just imported a kilo of "cocaine pasta" from Colombia. He said: "I look simple and poor, but I have a good business and make enough money to go to the World Cup games in Spain." When I told him that I had met a lot of drug buyers and drug dealers in the Lurigancho prison, he was hardly impressed. It seemed that he worked for the drug underworld, and that he was so well protected that his frankness about this business was not any real risk for him.

Besides this drug dealer, there were many others who wanted to tell me their stories, some jokingly, others seriously, some heavily inebriated, others with a clear mind. What struck me most of all was the easy way in which these Peruvians received me and let me be one of them.

More and more, the desire grows in me simply to walk around, greet people, enter their homes, sit on their doorsteps, play ball, throw water, and be known as someone who wants to live with them. It is a privilege to have the time and the freedom to practice this simple ministry of presence. Still, it is not as simple as it seems. My own desire to be useful, to do something significant, or to be part of some impressive project is so strong that soon my time is taken up by meetings, conferences, study groups, and workshops that prevent me from walking the streets. It is difficult not to have plans, not to organize people around an urgent cause, and not to feel that you are working directly for social progress. But I wonder more and more if the first thing shouldn't be to know people by name, to eat and to drink with them, to listen to their stories and tell your own, and to let them know with words, handshakes, and hugs that you do not simply like them, but truly love them.

If I ever decide to live in Peru for a long time, I think I should stay in one place and spend the first year doing little more than participating in the daily Peruvian life. A ministry of word and sacrament has to grow from a deep solidarity with the people. Contemplation is essential to ministry, and listening to people's lives and receiving them in a prayerful heart is true contemplation. I have little doubt that out of this contemplation it will become clear how the good news of the Gospel has to be announced, and how the healing presence of God needs to be made manifest among his people.

The greatest news of all is that God is with his people, that he is truly present. What greater ministry, then, can be practiced than a ministry that reflects this divine presence? And why worry? If God is with his own, his own will show me the way.

Monday, February 22

I am still fascinated with the question of what it would be like to be living with two or three brothers or sisters in the midst of one of the *barrios* of Lima, praying together at regular hours, walking the streets, visiting the homes, spending one day in study and reflection, practicing hospitality whenever possible, and celebrating the mysteries of God's presence. The core of this idea is that of living among the people to learn from them. This might sound romantic and sentimental, but in fact it requires discipline to allow the people to become our teachers. With such discipline, all that we see and hear can become a rich source for locating the presence of God among his people.

It would be a ministry of presence, but an active, articulate, considered presence. It would be a mutual ministry of continuous receiving and giving. It would be contemplation and action, cele-

bration and liberation, study and work, ascetic and festive, fraternal and hospitable. I am convinced that there are at this moment
young, idealistic, well-trained theological students who would be
very open to such a ministry. Is this idea a dream, a fantasy, an
illusion, or something worth pursuing? I will let it rest for a while
and see what happens with this little seed that I put into the
ground of my own search to serve God.

Tuesday, February 23

Villa Salvador is a section of Lima that in 1971 was nothing but
a bare desert, dry, sandy, isolated, and inhospitable. Now, eleven
years later, three hundred thousand people have found a home
there. It has been a hard and painful struggle for the people to
make the desert into a city, but now they are proud of what they
have accomplished. There is a water supply, electricity, many
schools, and a slowly improving transportation system that takes
the workers to their factories and offices.

Today I visited Eugene Kirk, an Irish priest who has lived in
Villa Salvador for the last eight years. I also visited two "little
brothers of Jesus," the Frenchman Jacinto and the Basque José,
who founded one of their fraternities there. What most struck me
during the long conversations with Eugene, Jacinto, and José was
that they considered the simple act of staying with the people the
core of their ministry. Eugene began in Villa Salvador by living in
a small shack and setting up a little carpentry shop. Slowly but
surely he got to know many people and was able to build a Christian community that today is strong and vital. Jacinto works in a
small furniture factory and commutes two hours a day with thousands of others. José works in a carpenter's shop in the neighborhood. During the weekends, Jacinto and José stay around the
house to receive visitors and help the neighbors with whatever
needs they have. Eugene, Jacinto, and José have small chapels in
their houses and live as contemplatives in the midst of a sea of
humans.

It was a joy to spend a day with these men. They are simple,
good men who enjoy their life with the people immensely. They
work hard, yet they seem to have time for anyone and anything.
They feel at home in this desert-city and they speak easily about
the great privilege of being allowed to live and work as members
of the community of Villa Salvador.

There is a great and holy mystery here, the mystery of the incarnation lived in simple ways. I saw an Irishman, a Basque, and a Frenchman thanking and praising God daily for being given the opportunity to be with the people of God. The many little children walking in and out of their dwellings made me realize how close the Lord is to all of them.

Wednesday, February 24

Ash Wednesday. During the last weeks, I have slowly become aware of what my Lenten practice might be. It might be the development of some type of "holy indifference" toward the many small rejections I am subject to, and a growing attachment to the Lord and his passion.

I am constantly surprised at how hard it is for me to deal with the little rejections that people inflict on each other day by day. I feel this even more strongly now that I am living in a country where I am so dependent on introductions and invitations. It is hard to meet people, to see projects, or to learn about current issues if you are not explicitly brought in touch with them. During the last month, I kept hearing about many interesting events only when they were past! Why didn't anyone tell me about them? Why wasn't I invited? Why was nobody willing to make me aware of them? How should *I* know? I do not think that there is any hostility towards me. Everyone thinks that everyone knows, and nobody takes the initiative to extend a personal invitation. Thus I feel welcome and not welcome at the same time. Nobody objects to my presence, but nobody is very glad about it either.

This atmosphere often leaves me with a feeling of being rejected and left alone. When I swallow these rejections, I get quickly depressed and lonely; then I am in danger of becoming resentful and even vengeful. But it is such an institutional problem that I can hardly imagine that I can ever be without it. The Catholic Church, wherever I have seen it operate, from the Vatican to the parishes in the *barrios* of Peru, tends to make the personal subservient to the institutional. There is always a need for priests to say Masses, baptize, and marry, and anyone who can do that in a responsible way is always "welcome." There are so many things to do that good workers can easily be placed. At the same time, there are so many people asking for services, so many activities to participate in and meetings to attend, that it is difficult to pay attention to the intimate interpersonal aspects of existence. And thus the paradox becomes that those who preach love and defend the values of family life, friendship, and mutual support find themselves often living lonely lives in busy rectories.

Is there a solution to this? When I see the people I am working with, I doubt there is one. They are all deeply committed, hardworking, and caring people. They will all give their lives for their people. They are full of enthusiasm and pastoral energy. But they too are part of an enormous institution that has such a pervasive influence on their way of being that it is practically impossible to escape the loneliness it breeds.

But maybe all of this is the other side of a deep mystery, the mystery that we have no lasting dwelling place on this earth and that only God loves us the way we desire to be loved. Maybe all these small rejections are reminders that I am a traveler on the way to a sacred place where God holds me in the palm of his hand. Maybe I do have to become a little more indifferent towards all these ups and downs, ins and outs, of personal relationships and learn to rest more deeply in him who knows and loves me more than I know and love myself.

Thursday, February 25

Today, I realized that the question of where to live and what to do is really insignificant compared to the question of how to keep the eyes of my heart focused on the Lord. I can be teaching at Yale, working in the bakery at the Genesee Abbey, or walking around with poor children in Peru and feel totally useless, miserable, and depressed in all these situations. I am sure of it, because it has happened. There is not such a thing as the right place or the right job. I can be happy and unhappy in all situations. I am sure of it, because I have been. I have felt distraught and joyful in situations of abundance as well as poverty, in situations of popularity and anonymity, in situations of success and failure. The difference was never based on the situation itself, but always on my state of mind and heart. When I knew that I was walking with the Lord, I always felt happy and at peace. When I was entangled in my own complaints and emotional needs, I always felt restless and divided.

It is a simple truth that comes to me in a time when I have to decide about my future. Coming to Lima or not for five, ten, or twenty years is no great decision. Turning fully, unconditionally, and without fear to the Lord *is.* I am sure this awareness sets me free to look around here without much worrying and binds me to the holy call to pray unceasingly.

Friday, February 26

Rose Dominique and Rose Timothy, two Maryknoll sisters, are the directors of a small downtown office, the Centro de Creatividad y Cambio (The Center for Creativity and Change). Their work could be seen as a nonecclesiastical ministry through which they reach many different groups of people, non-Christians as well as Christians. This center is a grass-roots organization to work for a new society. Its members publish pamphlets and booklets to draw attention to urgent problems concerning health, education, and youth, and to suggest strategies for change. The "Roses" pay special attention to the plight of Peruvian women. They felt that working within the traditional church structures was not the best way to strive for the liberation of women; so they set up shop for themselves while continuing to offer their services to parishes and church groups when asked.

This morning I talked for an hour with Sister Rose Dominique. Her sharp and compassionate understanding of the Peruvian situation helped me to articulate some of my own feelings of which I had been only vaguely aware. What impressed me most was her observation that the leaders in the theology of liberation had little sympathy with or understanding of the issues that touch the oppressed situation of the women in the church. Rose remarked: "In this Catholic country, it is very hard to change the predominantly clerical way in which the Church works. The liberation theologians are very much Church people, and they have a hard time considering our concern for women as a real part of their struggle for liberation."

I feel that she was talking about something that I had noticed but had found hard to pinpoint. The obvious and overwhelming need for socioeconomic liberation and the undeniable presence of immense poverty creates a situation in which women's issues are easily seen as a distraction, especially in a clerical, male-dominated Church. I had felt this in many little ways. After living for many years in an interdenominational and interconfessional setting, I could feel the strong dominating influence of a Church that is the only real religious power. And even the most progressive and liberated people in that Church are still marked, mostly unconsciously, by this clerical, male-dominated way of thinking and living.

Saturday, February 27

During the last few weeks I have been asking myself and others if I was learning enough about pastoral ministry during my stay in Pamplona Alta. I love the family I live with, I enjoy celebrating the Eucharist with the people, I am moved when I bring Communion to the sick, and I appreciate my weekly meetings with the lectors, but I have not really become a part of the pastoral team. Most things that happen remain unknown to me, and somehow I am getting the message that it is more a bother than a help to make me part of the daily life of the parish. I had hoped to participate in youth-group meetings, to visit the little communities in some of the sections of the parish, to help out in preparations for the sacraments of baptism and matrimony and —in general—to share actively in the ministry of the parish. Now I feel that I am standing in the center of a busy square wondering in which direction everyone is going. Last week I discussed my feelings with Tom, but it seems hard to make me part of things.

The whole situation is quite understandable. People are busy, and there are so many short-term visitors that it becomes fatiguing to keep introducing them over and over again to the daily goings-on in the parish. I have come to the conclusion that I have learned as much as I can and that I had better try to discover some new areas of ministry outside of Pamplona Alta before I leave Peru. In order to be able to make a responsible decision about my future, I need more experience than I can get here.

So this afternoon I explained to Charles and Tom that I felt it was better to move back to the center house in Miraflores and to start visiting people and places from there. It was hard to say good-bye to Sophia, Johnny, Pablito, and Maria. Living with them was, undoubtedly, the most important experience of my time here. Their affection and friendship were gifts for which I will always remain grateful. We ate some ice cream together, and Johnny and Pablito helped me carry my suitcases to the bus. When I stood on the steps of the bus and saw them waving good-bye, I felt a real pain and prayed that somehow I would be able to see them again as happy and mature adults. I waved back and shouted: *"Adiós, hasta la vista, gracias por todo."*

Sunday, February 28

This morning at 11:00 I had a good visit with Bishop Herman Schmidt, one of the auxiliary bishops of Lima. His main responsibility is the young towns in the southern part of Lima. I wanted to express to him some of the ideas that have developed in my mind during the last month and get his response. I explained my desire to live in a poor section of Lima—alone or with a few others—and to try to articulate the rich spiritual gifts of the people. My short stay with Sophia, Pablo, and their children had given me a glimpse of the presence of God with the poor. What a joy it would be to make this divine presence visible not only to them but also to the many nonpoor people who sincerely search for light in their darkness! A life of prayer and hospitality among the poor, to discover and express their gifts, is slowly presenting itself as a vocation to me.

Bishop Schmidt responded warmly, even enthusiastically, to this idea. But he felt that something more was needed. He said: "There is such a need for spiritual growth and formation among the poor that you would offer a real service with retreats and days of recollection for the people. They are too tied down to their homes to travel far for days of reflection and study. But if an opportunity for this arose in their own neighborhood, they would gladly respond." Bishop Schmidt kept stressing that his idea was not really different from mine. He only wanted to "complete the picture" based on his own understanding of the need of the people.

I felt affirmed in this conversation, and I have a sense that something is becoming visible that might prove to be more than just a fantasy. Bishop Schmidt suggested that I discuss my ideas a little more with others, and then present them to the Cardinal of Lima. He made it clear that he could not yet give his permission and that the Cardinal needed to be consulted before any action was taken. But that is not my problem at this time. I am far from that phase. At this moment I was happy to have a sympathetic response from a Peruvian bishop.

6.

M A R C H

The Outlines of a Vision

Monday, March 1

Sister Rebecca, one of the Marist sisters, took me this morning to Larco Herrera, a huge mental hospital in Lima. Rebecca had worked in the Lurigancho prison, and also had access to the pavilion of the mentally ill prisoners who are sent to this hospital.

We spent most of the morning with Manuel and Luis, two prisoner-patients. Both are intelligent and articulate people who in no way showed any signs of being criminals or mentally ill. They took us around their pavilion, introduced us to their fellow inmates, and explained everything we wanted to know. We also spoke with the psychologist of the section, a friendly man who received us and our guides with great hospitality and discussed the difficult situation of his patients. Most of them were never sentenced, and nobody could say how long they would remain locked up. We also talked a bit to the *guardia republicana,* the armed guards who surround this little section of the hospital, since it is a prison as well.

Although the place, which houses thirty-eight patients, was extremely poor; although the patients had nothing to keep them busy; although the justice system in Peru is so bureaucratic and complex that these men may be there for many years without any attention to their case, the atmosphere was very humane. Guards, doctors, and patients treated each other amiably, talked freely, and showed a remarkable openness to each other. Somehow, the Peruvian friendliness and hospitality have taken some of the sharp edges off the suffering of these men. One of the guards even allowed Luis to bring us to the main gate. He walked along with us and was as much a part of the party as Rebecca, Luis, and myself.

Poverty, injustice, misery, and loneliness were all present; but in the midst of it all I saw an expression of humanity I have never seen in any mental hospital before. While we walked to the gate, I noticed that Luis was playing with scissors and a piece of silver paper from a pack of cigarettes. Just before we said good-bye, he offered me a lovely silver flower that he had quickly made while walking. This gesture captured the poignancy and paradox of my visit. I embraced him and for a moment all was good, very good.

Tuesday, March 2

This morning I visited the Centro Bartolome de las Casas with Bill McCarthy. A three-story building on Ricardo Bentin street in Rimac, it is the heart of the liberation theology movement. I had heard so much about it that I expected a large building, with many people and classrooms, full of activity. Instead, I saw a very simple house in a suburb of Lima. Gustavo Gutiérrez, who founded the center, was not in; but Alberto Maguina, one of the staff members, received us kindly and told us all we wanted to know.

The center is an independent institute with a small staff of sociologists and theologians who dedicate themselves to socio-theological studies and to the formation and continuing education of pastoral agents in Peru. Their work is divided into four main areas: (1) popular religiosity; (2) the daily life of the poor; (3) the poor as protagonists of their own history; and (4) Church and Society. Under these four titles, different subjects are studied.

One of the subjects under the heading of "popular religiosity" is "the moral sense of the poor." Such a theme is prepared by the staff in a pre-workshop, in which all the available literature is studied and methodological questions are dealt with. Then a year-long workshop is set up, in which about forty people participate. These people are mostly grass-roots workers, men and women who live and work with the poor and can offer their observations and experience as sources for reflection. After a year, the results of the workshops are summarized and made available to a larger circle of pastoral workers. Some of the work of the center finds its way into *Páginas,* the widely read monthly magazine edited by Carmen Lora, or in the publications of Centro de Estudios y Publicaciones (CEP), directed by Pedro de Guchtenere.

What is most striking about this center of higher studies is that it stays close to the daily life of the people. It practices theology by reflecting critically on socioeconomic, political, and ecclesiastical events, and by evaluating these events in the light of the Gospel and the teachings of the Church. There is a large library of classical theological sources and documents of past and present events in Church and state. It is clear that these are continually consulted and studied with the concrete problems of the day in mind.

What makes liberation theology so original, challenging, and radical is not so much its conceptual content as its method of working. A true liberation theologian is not just someone who thinks about liberation, but someone whose thought grows out of a life of solidarity with those who are poor and oppressed. The most impressive aspect of the Centro Bartolome de las Casas is that those who come and work there are men and women whose knowledge has grown from an intimate participation in the daily life of the people who struggle for freedom. Thus the center reveals one of the oldest of truths: that *theologia* is not primarily a way of thinking, but a way of living. Liberation theologians do not think themselves into a new way of living, but live themselves into a new way of thinking.

Wednesday, March 3

This morning I had a pleasant discussion with David Molineau, the new director of *Noticias Aliadas* (Latin American Press). I mentioned to David how impressed I had been with the way the Peruvian people express their faith, their gratitude, their care, their hopes, and their love. I told him that it might be a special task for me to give words to much of the spiritual richness that I saw, but of which the people themselves are hardly aware. David agreed, but added: "Living with the poor not only makes you see the good more clearly, but the evil as well." He told me some stories from his own experience in a Peruvian parish, and illustrated the truth that in a world of poverty, the lines between darkness and light, good and evil, destructiveness and creativity, are much more distinct than in a world of wealth.

One of the temptations of upper-middle-class life is to create large gray areas between good and evil. Wealth takes away the sharp edges of our moral sensitivities and allows a comfortable confusion about sin and virtue. The difference between rich and poor is not that the rich sin more than the poor, but that the rich find it easier to call sin a virtue. When the poor sin, they call it sin; when they see holiness, they identify it as such. This intuitive clarity is often absent from the wealthy, and that absence easily leads to the atrophy of the moral sense.

David helped me see that living with the poor does not keep me away from evil, but it does allow me to see evil in sharper, clearer ways. It does not lead me automatically to the good either, but will help me see good in a brighter light, less hidden and more convincing. Once I can see sin and virtue with this clarity, I will also see sadness and joy, hatred and forgiveness, resentment and gratitude in less nebulous ways.

Thursday, March 4

Not far from the Maryknoll center house is the secretariat of the Latin American section of Pax Romana. This large Catholic student organization is hardly known in the United States, but in Latin America it is one of the most creative and influential forces in recent developments in the Church. Many of the leaders of the liberation theology movement, laymen, laywomen, and priests, received their spiritual formation and inspiration through membership in Pax Romana. For many years, Gustavo Gutiérrez has been the chaplain of UNEC, the Peruvian section of Pax Romana, and layleaders such as Manuel Piqueras, Xavier Iguiniz, and Rolando Ames had and still have intimate ties with this Catholic student movement.

I had lunch with the staff today. There were representatives from Brazil, Ecuador, the Dominican Republic, Chile, Spain, and Peru. They told me that I would never understand the meaning and influence of liberation theology without seeing the Catholic student movement as an integral part of its growth. After lunch I talked to Luis Maria Goicoechea, a Basque priest. He told me about the history of Pax Romana, showed me its publication, and gave me some idea of the preparations for the upcoming assembly in Montreal, where the emphasis will be on the poor in the world.

The core of the spirituality of Pax Romana is *La Revisión de Vida,* an ongoing process of evaluation of one's daily life in the light of the Gospel. It is an important discipline that challenges the members to explore how they live out their Christian commitment in the concrete events of each day. The question, "How did I put my life in service of the Kingdom of God today?" invites the active members of the movement (they call themselves *militantes*) to continue to develop, and search for new directions. It is this spiritual flexibility that made it possible for the Latin American Pax Romana to play such a crucial role in the years that followed Vatican II.

Friday, March 5

It is far from easy to be a missioner. One has to live in a different culture, speak a different language, and get used to a different climate, all at great distances from those patterns of life which fit most comfortably. It is not surprising that, for many missioners, life is full of tension, frustration, confusion, anxiety, alienation, and loneliness.

Why do people become missioners? Why do they leave what is familiar and known to live in a milieu that is unfamiliar and unknown? This question has no simple answer. A desire to serve Christ unconditionally, an urge to help the poor, an intellectual interest in another culture, the attraction of adventure, a need to break away from family, a critical insight into the predicament of one's own country, a search for self-affirmation—all these and many other motives can be part of the making of a missioner. Long and arduous formation offers the opportunity for re-alignment and purification of these motives. A sincere desire to work in the service of Jesus Christ and his kingdom should become increasingly central in the mind and heart of a future missioner, although nobody can be expected to be totally altruistic. Not seldom do we come in touch with our hidden drives only after long and hard work in the field. Preparatory formation and training cannot do everything. The issue is not to have perfectly motivated missioners, but missioners who are willing to be purified again and again as they struggle to find their true vocation in life.

The two most damaging motives in the makeup of missioners seem to be guilt and the desire to save. Both form the extremes of a long continuum, both make life in the mission extremely painful. As long as I go to a poor country because I feel guilty about my wealth, whether financial or mental, I am in for a lot of trouble. The problem with guilt is that it is not taken away by work. Hard work for the poor may push my guilt underground for a while, but can never really take it away. Guilt has roots deeper than can be reached through acts of service. On the other hand, the desire to save people from sin, from poverty, or from exploitation can be just as harmful, because the harder one tries the more one is confronted with one's own limitations. Many hardworking men and women have seen the situation getting worse during their missionary career; and if they depended solely on the success of their work, they would quickly lose their sense of self-worth. Although a sense of guilt and a desire to save can be very destructive and depressive for missioners, I do not think that we are ever totally free from either. We feel guilty and we desire to bring about change. These experiences will always play a part in our daily life.

The great challenge, however, is to live and work out of gratitude. The Lord took on our guilt and saved us. In him the Divine work has been accomplished. The human missionary task is to give visibility to the Divine work in the midst of our daily existence. When we can come to realize that our guilt has been taken away and that only God saves, then we are free to serve, then we can live truly humble lives. Clinging to guilt is resisting God's grace, wanting to be a savior, competing with God's own being. Both are forms of idolatry and make missionary work very hard and eventually impossible.

Humility is the real Christian virtue. It means staying close to the ground *(humus)*, to people, to everyday life, to what is happening with all its down-to-earthness. It is the virtue that opens our eyes for the presence of God on the earth and allows us to live grateful lives. The poor themselves are the first to help us recognize true humility and gratitude. They can make a receptive missioner a truly happy person.

Saturday, March 6

Today I met Xavier Iguiniz. During the last few weeks, I had heard his name mentioned different times, always with great respect and sympathy. Xavier is professor of Economics at the Catholic University in Lima, and a very committed and active collaborator of the Centro Bartolome de las Casas. He has known Gustavo Gutiérrez since his years as a student, and has become increasingly involved in the liberation theology movement.

One of the most interesting things Xavier said to me was that liberation theology was a way of thinking and working in close relationship with and in obedience to the *movimiento popular,* the movement of the people. He contrasted the individualistic academic world that I come from, characterized by the principles of competition and "publish or perish," with the slow, patient, and communal way of working of the people who meet at the Centro Bartolome de las Casas.

"We are not interested in creating a new theology, we are not trying to confront traditional church structures. We are not hoping for quick radical changes. No, we want to listen carefully and patiently to the movement of the people and slowly identify those elements that lead to progress. We want to work as church participants in an age-old process of living, thinking, celebrating, and worshiping, and then give form and shape to what really belongs to the movement of God's people."

Xavier was very aware of the fact that he belonged to the Church, which works slowly and gradually but in which sudden eruptions can make drastic change possible. Such eruptions, although they cannot be organized, need to be recognized, understood, evaluated, and made part of the larger movement of the Church. "We have thousands of ideas, insights, and visions. We talk about them, exchange them, and play with them. Often they seem very significant, but most of them are shelved, usually for many years. A few of these ideas, insights, and visions may later reappear and prove to be substantial. But it can be a long time before we know if we are in touch with something that really belongs to the movement."

Xavier showed me—without explicitly saying so—a theology of doing theology. He was extremely critical of "theological heroism." He did not believe in simply publishing all the good ideas that come up. He kept stressing the need for humble, slow, faithful work in obedience to the people who are to be served. He said: "Many of the poor are still very close to the Council of Trent in their spirituality. If we do not understand this, our concern for their liberation cannot be a true Christian service."

Xavier was sympathetic to my desire to live with the people, but strongly urged me to continue my academic work. The greatest need, he felt, was not for more pastoral workers but for people who could help articulate, evaluate, systematize, and communicate what is going on in the pastoral field. "We need people who can conceptualize what they live and connect it with the larger tradition of the Church." He warned me against romanticism: "It is quite possible to live with the people without being part of the movement of the people, and that movement you might find as much in the university as in the *barrio.*"

My general impression was that Xavier did not discourage me in my desire to come to Peru, but he did want to make me aware that the way of doing theology here would require a great faithfulness to the slow-moving Church of the people.

Sunday, March 7

Rose Timothy and Rose Dominique invited me to come to Caja de Agua, a large barrio in the North Zone of Lima where they live. I arrived at 8:00 A.M. and went straight to the rectory. There I met Mattias Sienbenaller, the pastor of Caja de Agua and the Vicar of the whole North Zone. Mattias is a diocesan priest from Luxembourg who has worked in Lima for the last sixteen years. He is highly respected and admired by many and has been a creative and patient leader since he arrived in Peru.

Mattias had not the faintest idea who this poorly-Spanish-speaking stranger was that walked into his house at 8:00 A.M. on Sunday morning. He seemed suspicious in the beginning, and didn't know how to respond. He offered me a cup of coffee and asked many questions. After awhile, he relaxed and showed interest in my search for a vocation in Peru. He said that he had very little time for me at this moment, but invited me to come back and stay with him for a few days so that he could give me a better perspective on the possibilities of coming to Peru. He felt that my experience so far had been far too limited, and that I needed a broader vision to be able to make a responsible decision.

I immediately realized that I had met a man who has much to offer. Since he is a diocesan priest from Europe—as I am—with much experience in Peru, I felt a strong desire to spend more time with him.

Monday, March 8
Cuzco, Peru

During these last weeks, the Maryknollers Michael Briggs and Paul Kavanaugh were staying in the Center house. Both are working in the Altiplano, the high mountain plane around Lake Titicaca, and have come to Lima for their altitude leave, a much-needed time to recuperate from the physical stresses of "high living."

Talking with them has increased my desire to see more of Peru than Lima. They convinced me that to know only Lima would give me a very one-sided impression, not only of Peru, but also of the pastoral work in Peru. Before returning to their missions, Mike and Paul planned to attend a two-week course in Cuzco for all the pastoral workers of the region of the Southern Andes. They invited me to join them.

So this morning we flew from Lima to Cuzco and settled in at the Instituto Pastoral Andino (the Pastoral Institute of the Andes). Since the course does not start until tomorrow morning, I had the whole day to look around Cuzco. Cuzco is like a precious pearl set in a lovely green valley. The many trees, the fresh pastures, and the green-covered mountains offered a dramatic change from the dry and dusty hills of Pamplona Alta. Set in the pure blue sky, a bright sun threw its light over the small city. The central square of Cuzco is of unusual beauty. The imposing facades of the cathedral and the Church of the Compañia are flanked by pleasant galleries with shops, restaurants, bars, and bookstores.

Paul and I walked around town for a few hours and enjoyed the busy life in this Quechua town. The dark faces of the people, the stores with beautiful Indian handicrafts, the old Inca walls in which huge stones interlock with meticulous precision, and the many memories of the Inca empire all made me aware that Cuzco explains much of the glory and agony of present-day Peru.

In the late afternoon we took a cab to the Indian ruins surrounding the city. We saw the old Inca fortress of Sacsahuamán, the sculpted rock of Quenkko, and the ritual baths of Tambomachay. These solemn and sacred sights in the midst of splendid green mountains gave me the desire to spend some quiet days there meditating on the mystery and misery of human history. I soon realized that the splendid churches in downtown Cuzco were built with the stones from these old Indian temples and fortresses. The main concern of the Spaniards had been to destroy the pagan world and to show triumphantly the victory of the Christian faith. The Indian people were only reluctantly recognized as human beings. It would take centuries to acknowledge their rich spiritual heritage. Only recently has mission come to mean something other than a spiritual conquest.

In Cuzco, all can be seen together: the solemn faces of the Inca gods, the glory and the shame of a Christianity proclaimed with the support of the sword, the living faith of the people who have brought their Indian heritage and their new religion together into a deeply rooted spirituality, and the poverty and oppression of a people that has never fully regained its freedom.

Tuesday, March 9

Rolando Ames, a political scientist at the Catholic University in Lima, is leading the first three days of the course. The lectures are on the *Coyuntura Política Eclesiástica,* the status of Church and politics in Peru.

In his brilliant lectures, Rolando brought together many of the pieces of information, insight, hearsay, and gossip that I had gathered during the last two months. Many things fell into place. Rolando described the years 1976 to 1978 as the period during which a new revolutionary consciousness developed that affected the whole nation. This new consciousness provided the climate for a new way to preach the gospel and deeply influenced the pastoral work of the Peruvian Church. This period has now passed. Today the Church has to continue to work in a different political climate. With the popular movement no longer as clearly visible, an increasing pragmatism has emerged that makes the poor less militant and the left less clear about its direction.

Rolando affirmed in a concrete way what Xavier told me on Saturday, namely that it is crucial for every pastoral worker to keep in close touch with the political ups and downs of Peru. The problems of 1971 and those of 1982 might look much the same; there is still poverty, malnutrition, lack of educational facilities, poor medical care, and a great need for a more developed knowledge of the Christian faith. Why, then, is there a need to enter into the complexity of daily politics? Rolando's answer is that even when the problems seem the same, the spiritual tone can be very different. The understanding of this tone is essential for the work of a Christian who really wants to serve the people. To ignore the political movements of a country such as Peru is to ignore the realities that determine the hope or despair of the people.

During the past few years, Peru has shifted toward a growing dependence on international capitalism. All the emphasis is on promoting export of those materials that serve the needs of the large transnational corporations. This means less support for local and national enterprises, and thus less work and money for Peruvian workers and companies. Since the transnational corporations don't see any profit coming from capital invested in people's projects (educational, agrarian, or industrial) these "economics" offer little optimism to the people.

How then can we form true communities of hope in the midst of this political reality? That is the question that touches the heart of pastoral care in this country.

Wednesday, March 10

Rolando Ames helped us to identify today the major developments within the Peruvian Church over the last thirty years. In many ways, they reflect the tumultuous events within the Church in all of Latin America.

Three main phases can be distinguished. First of all, the Church distanced itself from the ruling class—or the oligarchy, as it is called in Latin America. Until the fifties, the Latin American Church lived and worked hand in glove with the ruling class. The *haciendas,* where owner and priest were both considered as bosses by those who worked the land, were vivid manifestation of the connection between the Church and the oligarchy. But in 1958, an official church document appeared in which the *orden oligárquico* (rule by oligarchy) was called unjust. It was the first sign of a movement in the Church that called attention to the plight of the poor and oppressed.

In the second phase, the Church moved from a general sympathy for the poor to an active defense of their rights. The Vatican Council had set the tone which made this development possible, but the Conference of the Latin American Bishops in Medellin in 1968 gave it shape. In Medellin, the Church formulated the "preferential option for the poor" and thus defined itself as a Church that supports oppressed people in their struggle for liberation. In many ways, the statements of Medellin went far beyond the psychological state of mind of most of the bishops there present. But the decision by the Church as a body to speak directly and officially in defense of the poor, oppressed, and exploited peoples of Latin America meant the birth of a new Church. By calling the order that causes the rampant injustices "sinful," the Church had committed itself—at least in principle—to the struggle for a new social order.

This radical change in self-definition made the Latin American Church of the seventies a Church drenched by the blood of martyrs. In Argentina, Brazil, Chile, El Salvador, Guatemala, and many other countries, thousands of Christians lost their lives as a consequence of their commitment to this new Church. Although direct persecution did not take place in Peru, the option for the poor has led to many conflicts between the Church and the Peruvian ruling class.

The third phase has just begun, the phase in which an ecclesial counter-reaction is taking shape. During the seventies, the opposition within the Church itself against a new direction had remained dormant. But in the beginning of the eighties, a new and well-organized conservatism that divides the Church into two camps has become visible. One of the preparatory documents for the Latin American Bishops' Conference in Puebla, published in 1979, opened this third phase. The document describes the task of the Church as guiding the unavoidable transition of the Latin American society from a rural to an industrial society. It stressed the necessity of preventing the secularism that resulted from a similar transition in France during the last century, and it pointed to the bishops of Latin America as those who have to secure the faith in this time of change.

Today, the conservative forces in the Church in Peru are well-established. Because the hierarchy can no longer follow one line, the episcopal documents have become compromises between two opposing directions. Whereas, a few years ago, the Peruvian bishops could still issue strongly prophetic statements in the spirit of Medellin, the latest publications of the Peruvian Bishops' Conference show ambiguity, ambivalence, and paralysis.

Rolando showed how hard it will be for many who found their faith in the new church to continue in the struggle and not become discouraged. But he was convinced that the new conservatism is a passing phase to test and purify the new commitment to the poor, from which there is no return.

Friday, March 12

Tonight George-Ann Potter, assistant director of Catholic Relief Services in Peru, invited me to dinner. She also invited Rolando

Ramos, a Peruvian priest who works in Amparaes (Calca province). Although I had never met (or even heard of) Rolando, an immediate sense of friendship developed between us. It seemed to me that here was the priest I had been looking for. He combined a deep, contemplative spirit with a strong commitment to service among the poor. He radiated faith in the presence of God among the people, hope for the liberation of the poor, and love for all he meets. Being in his presence felt like being in the presence of a man of God, a pastor and prophet.

Rolando's parish is four hours away from Cuzco. He serves a large group of small villages that can be reached only on horseback or on foot. He lives the life of the poor and participates fully in their daily struggles. He lives this hard life with gladness, because he can see, hear, and touch the Lord in his people and feels deeply grateful for that privilege.

I guess that my joy in knowing Rolando has something to do with my difficulties in relating to the people in the course. I find the participants tough and even harsh. They have so identified themselves with the *lucha* that they permit little space for personal interchange. They are good and honest people, but difficult to get to know. They work diligently, not only in their parishes but also in this course. They are serious, intense, and deeply concerned men and women.

When I met Rolando and experienced his personal warmth, his kindness, and his spiritual freedom, I was suddenly able to come in touch with the feelings of oppression that I myself was experiencing in the course. Rolando invited me to come to his parish and to live with him for as long as I wanted. There I would be able to experience that it was possible to be fully involved in the struggle for the poor while at the same time remaining sensitive to the personal and interpersonal quality of life. That explains my immediate feelings of closeness to him.

Saturday, March 13

For the last few days, the course has dealt primarily with the new agricultural law. A lawyer from Lima came to explain the law, and triggered a lively debate about the way the poor *campesinos* would be affected by it. Most pastoral workers felt that this law was simply one more way in which the poor would be made poorer. The law opened the way for rich people who had lost their land during the agrarian reform to reclaim it. One of the French pastoral workers presented an alternative law that would serve the poor farmer. This law had been formulated by the *campesinos* themselves, with the help of leftist lawyers and economists.

When I reflect on these legal debates and discussions, I become strongly aware of the new style of this liberation-oriented Church. It would have taken an outsider a long time to find out that this was a group of priests, nuns, and Catholic laymen and laywomen dedicated to the preaching of the Gospel. The style of the dialogue, the fervor of the discussions, and the ideological language suggested a meeting of a political party rather than a church group. I feel that this is true not only for the formal sessions, but also for the informal relationships between the participants—during meals and coffee breaks. Yet these men and women from France, Spain, Italy, and the United States have left their countries to serve the poor of Peru in the name of the Lord Jesus Christ. Their religious dedication has led them into the lives of the poor. Therefore the sophisticated and highly critical analysis of the new agrarian law was for them not purely political but a necessary step in the struggle for freedom for the people of God.

Yet two Churches are gradually developing in Peru, and they are at the point where they are no longer able to talk to each other. On the one side is the Church that speaks primarily about God, with little reference to the daily reality in which the people live; on the other side is the Church that speaks primarily about the struggle of the people for freedom, with little reference to the Divine mysteries to which this struggle points. The distance between these Churches is growing. This morning I went to the Cathedral of Cuzco, and when I walked from altar to altar and statue to statue and listened to the monotone voice of a priest saying Mass, I suddenly felt a deep pain. I would never feel at home any more in this traditional Church, but will I ever in the Church of the *lucha*?

Sunday, March 14

George-Ann Potter and her guest, Anne Lise Timmerman, vice-president of Caritas in Denmark, invited me to join them on a trip to the sacred valley of the Incas.

The majestic beauty of this valley impressed me; the Urubamba

River, surrounded by fertile cornfields and green-covered mountain ranges, filled me with awe. Along the road small groups of Indians guiding cattle carried their loads of wood. These small, dark, silent people with faces carved by nature and hard work evoked in me a sense of the sacred.

In their silence, they spoke of centuries of care for the land, of a mysterious intimacy with nature, of an unceasing prayer to the God who has made their land fertile, and of a knowledge that we in our Volkswagen would never be able to grasp. The valley was filled with a holy silence: no advertisements along the roads, no factories or modern houses, no loudspeakers or shouting vendors. Even the busy market of the little town of Pisac seemed covered with this sacred quietness.

We bought a few artifacts in the marketplace, attended Mass in the Pisac Church, and visited an agricultural school for *campesinos*. We talked about all sorts of things, had a pleasant dinner, and struggled for an hour to change a tire. But none of our activity could disturb the sacred silence of this valley of the Incas. When we came back to Cuzco I felt refreshed, renewed, and grateful to the Indian people for this healing gift of silence.

Monday, March 15

Today the last part of the course began. After three days about the political and ecclesial state of affairs in Peru, and two days about the new agrarian law and its possible alternatives, the emphasis now shifts to a spirituality of liberation. Gustavo Gutiérrez flew into Cuzco from Lima this morning, and will be our guide in a four-day workshop. Just as in the summer course in Lima, Gustavo's presence had a vitalizing effect. Many of us showed signs of fatigue after six days of intense discussions, but Gustavo unleashed new energies and engendered new enthusiasm.

Two ideas in Gustavo's presentations impressed me deeply. The first focused on the Gospel terms, which have passed through the filter of individualism and thus have been spiritualized and sentimentalized. The word "poor" has come to mean "humble," the word "rich," "proud." Terms like "the children," "the blind," "the sinner" have lost their historical meaning and have been "translated" into ahistorical, asocial and apolitical words. Thus, "child," which in the New Testament refers to an insignificant, marginal, and oppressed human being, has become an expression for simplicity, innocence, and spontaneity. Jesus' call to become "like children" has been passed through the filter of individualism and has thus been romanticized.

This explains how the idea of a spiritual combat has lost its social, political, and economic quality and now refers only to an inner struggle. Gustavo showed us as an example of how the Magnificat is mostly read in a very individualistic way and has lost its radical, social dimensions in the minds of most contemporary Christians. In the Magnificat, Mary proclaims: "[The Lord God] has shown the strength of his arm, he has scattered the proud in their conceit. He has cast down the mighty from their thrones and has lifted up the lowly." These words have a concrete historical, socio-economic, and political meaning; the interpretations that relate these words exclusively to the inner life of pride and humility rob them of their real power.

A second idea that touched me in Gustavo's presentation was that affection, tenderness, solitude are not to be rejected by those who struggle for the freedom of the people. There is a danger that these important realities of the Christian life are considered by the "revolutionaries" as soft and useless for the struggle. But Gustavo made it clear that love for the people is essential for a true Christian revolution. Those who do not value tenderness and gentleness will eventually lose their commitment to the struggle for liberation.

This observation was extremely important to me, especially in the context of my earlier feelings about the participants in this course. Someone mentioned to me that "new fighters" in the struggle for liberation often are tense, harsh, and unfeeling, but that those who have been in the struggle for a long time are gentle, caring, and affectionate people who have been able to integrate the most personal with the most social. Gustavo himself is certainly an "old fighter."

Tuesday, March 16

Today Gustavo showed how the eruption of the poor has dramatic implications for our spirituality. The new and concrete pastoral concerns that came out of the involvement with the poor have dramatically challenged the traditional ways of living the spiritual life. But those who have gone through this crisis and tasted it to the full have also come to realize that, even though the experience of a break with the past remains a reality, so too does continuity. In fact, as Gustavo remarked, the full immersion in the struggle makes us rediscover the basic spiritual values that also undergirded the "old-fashioned" seminary spirituality. Humility, faithfulness, obedience, purity—these and many other traditional values are being rediscovered in the midst of the work with the poor.

One example of this rediscovery of traditional values is the renewed understanding of humility. In the spirituality of the past there was little place for conflict; but anyone who really becomes involved in the daily lives and struggles of the poor cannot avoid moments and periods of conflict. Experiences of abandonment, despair, and deep anguish can enter into the spiritual life itself. It can even lead to a struggle and confrontation with God, who does not seem to make his presence known. Thus a spirituality marked by the struggle for liberation can lead to an experience of deep darkness, which will require true humility. It is this humility that enables us to continue in the struggle, even when we see little progress, to be faithful even when we experience only darkness, to stay with the people even when we ourselves feel abandoned.

I am moved by this new understanding of humility, precisely because it is so old! It has deep connections with the humility of Jeremiah, who confronts God in the midst of his confusion, and with the humility of John of the Cross, who stays faithful in the darkness. Thus the new spirituality of liberation opens us to the mystical life as an essential part of the pastoral task given to us by the people themselves.

Wednesday, March 17

After lunch, I had an opportunity to spend some time with Gustavo Gutiérrez and to ask his advice about a possible long stay in Peru. He was extremely concrete in his advice. He said that it would be a good thing for me to come to Peru for a long time, live in a parish in Lima, do some pastoral work, get to know as much as possible the pastoral people of the city, and join a theological reflection group in the Centro Bartolome de las Casas. In many ways, his suggestions were similar to those of Xavier Iguiniz and Rolando Ames.

I feel far from making a decision of this nature. The many shifts in my emotions and my feelings of being a lonely bystander indicate that this is not the right time to accept Gustavo's invitation.

I am happy that I do not have to decide now, and that I can take more time to let things develop in me. It probably will be a gradual process of discernment. I will be at home here only when I experience my stay as a vocation, a call from God, and from the people. At this moment, the call is not clear. I will have to bring my search more directly into the presence of God and pray more fervently for light.

Thursday, March 18

Yesterday I read the so-called Santa Fe document. It is an analysis written in 1980 by a group of Latin American experts of the Republican Party, to formulate the new policy for the United States towards Latin America in anticipation of Ronald Reagan's presidency.

The third proposition of the second part reads: "The foreign policy of the United States must start to confront (and not simply respond after the facts) the theology of liberation as it is used in Latin America by the clergy of the 'liberation theology'."

This proposition is clarified by the following explanation:

> In Latin America, the role of the Church is vital for the concept of political freedom. Regrettably, the Marxist-Leninist forces have used the Church as a political weapon against private property and the capitalist system of production, by infiltrating the religious community with ideas which are more Communist than Christian (Translated from the French publication *Dial: diffusion de l'information sur l'Amérique Latine,* January 28, 1982).

Although these words show a lack of understanding of liberation theology, they disclose that those who were setting the guidelines for the greatest power in the world consider theology a real threat. The simple fact that theology is taken that seriously by people whose primary concern is to obtain and maintain first place among all the powers of the world is among the greatest compliments to theology I have ever heard.

There is a little man in Peru, a man without any power, who lives in a *barrio* with poor people and who wrote a book. In this book he simply reclaimed the basic Christian truth that God became human to bring good news to the poor, new light to the blind, and liberty to the captives. Ten years later this book and the movement it started are considered dangerous by the greatest power on earth. When I look at this little man, Gustavo, and think about the tall Ronald Reagan, I see David standing before Goliath again with no more weapon than a little stone, called *A Theology of Liberation.*

Friday, March 19

The Cuzco course is over. Last night we celebrated the Eucharist together in a way I will never forget. It was a celebration in which all the joys and the pains of the struggle for the liberation of the poor were brought together and lifted up together with the bread and the wine as a sacrifice of praise. It was a powerful spiritual experience, serious yet glad, realistic yet hopeful, very militant yet peaceful. It was for me the most prayerful moment of the course.

During his last presentation, Gustavo made an interesting observation. He remarked that the Christians of Latin America had passed from a traditional to a revolutionary understanding of their faith without going through a modernistic phase. One person in whom this process could be seen was Archbishop Oscar Romero of El Salvador. This traditional churchman became a true revolutionary through his direct contact with the suffering people without ever rejecting or even criticizing his traditional past. In fact, his traditional understanding of God's presence in history was the basis and source of his courageous protest against the exploitation and oppression of the people in El Salvador. What is true of Bishop Romero is true of most Latin American Christians who joined the movement for liberation. Their traditional understanding of the teachings of the Church was never a hindrance to their conversion. On the contrary, it was the basis for change.

Here we see an important difference between the Latin American situation and the situation in Western Europe and in some parts of the United States. Latin America did not go through a stage of secularization. In Europe, many liberation movements have an antireligious, antichurch, and anticlerical character. That is not the case today in Latin America. Most people who have joined liberation movements in Latin America are deeply believing Christians who look to the Church for guidance and support. Many Europeans who come to Latin America to know more about the people's movement for liberation are surprised and often impressed by the Christian commitment they encounter in the revolutionaries with whom they speak. Europeans often feel that the

175

Church has lost credibility and relevance in the struggle for a new world. But here they discover that the Church is one of the main sources of inspiration in the struggle.

The closing Eucharist of the course made this clear to me. The texts of Scripture, the prayers of petition and thanks, the offering of the gifts, the sharing of the bread and the cup, and the hymns of praise were an integral part of all that had been said during the last two weeks. The Eucharist was not tacked on to the course because all the participants were Christians. No, the Eucharist was the most powerful and the most radical expression of what this whole course was about. It became a powerful call to go out again and continue in the struggle of the people of God.

Saturday, March 20

Now that the course is finished, I am living with my Lutheran friends John and Kathy Goldstein in Cuzco.

It is wonderful to stay with friends in a "homey" house, to have a good bed, good conversation, and free time to write, to play with John and Kathy's five-week-old son, Peter Isaac, and to make little trips to the center of Cuzco. The difference between the intense atmosphere at the Pastoral Institute and the relaxed and friendly family atmosphere in the Goldstein's home has really struck me. It is the difference between quick meals on long tables with eighty people and leisurely meals around the kitchen table, between introducing yourself every moment to a new person and being in a familiar place, between always talking about Church and society and talking about the little things of daily life, between the hectic eagerness of celibates and the sustained concern of a father and a mother for their newborn child. All these differences make me very glad to be with my friends and to take it easy for a while.

Monday, March 22

During the last few days, I have been deeply disturbed by the news of the murder of four fellow Dutchmen in El Salvador. Koos Koster, Hans Lodewijk, Jan Kornelius Kuiper, and Johannes Willemsen were members of a Dutch television team sent to El Salvador to report on the political situation in the weeks before the elections. The radio mentions the official explanation of the Salvadoran government, which says that the four Dutchmen were caught in a crossfire between government troops and guerrilla fighters. The radio also mentions that another Dutch reporter refutes this explanation and says that the four were murdered by a military unit.

The Peruvian paper *El Diario* gives a detailed report of the murders. It says that the four Dutchmen had just finished their work and were on the way to the airport of Lloapango in their car, loaded with equipment and just-finished films. Near the detour of Santa Rosa, before the turn to Chalatenango, they were intercepted by a military truck. A group of soldiers of the fourth brigade of the infantry forced the four Dutchmen to board their truck, hitting them with the butts of their rifles. A little further, the prisoners were let out and machine-gunned down with total disregard for the astonished guides who accompanied the four Dutchmen and the people who witnessed the murder from the surrounding thicket. When the soldiers arrived in the *cuartel* of El Paisnal with the four bodies, they reported to their superiors. All the cameras, as well as films showing the daily agony of the Salvadoran people, were immediately destroyed.

In a long analysis of the murders, *El Diario* is of the opinion that "the Argentinian Colonels, who offer their intelligence service to the armed forces of El Salvador could finally rest since they had finished a hunt that had started nine years ago." With the help of Anibal Aguilar Penarrieta, the president of the Association of Lawyers for Human Rights in Bolivia, *El Diario* was able to reconstruct the journeys through Latin America of the Dutch television team during the last decade. Koos Koster was in Chile during the 1973 coup of General Augusto Pinochet and made an extraordinary film of the attack on the Palace de la Moneda, where President Salvador Allende died. During 1973, 1974, and 1975, Koster was in Peru with his colleagues and made films about the life of the *campesinos*. Later the team came to Argentina, where they made the best available documentary about the thirty thousand "disappeared ones" and the mothers of the Plaza de Mayo. When their shocking film appeared on European television, the Argentinian military started to look for an opportunity to kill them, according to *El Diario*. In 1980, the television crew was in Bolivia documenting the violations of human rights during the military occupation of the Bolivian tin mines. They also revealed the role of Argentina in the Bolivian coups of Garcia Meza and Arce Gomez. But when Arce Gomez ordered their arrest, they had already left Bolivia.

A few weeks ago, *El Diario* says the head of the Salvadoran armed forces traveled to Argentina to work out a plan for selective terrorism. Part of the conversation is supposed to have dealt with the way to eliminate the Dutch reporters in El Salvador. The plan was to authorize the Dutchmen to travel to the interior of El Salvador and to give them apparent freedom of movement. Then they would be arrested under the pretense that their names were found as contact persons on the dead body of a guerrilla fighter. *El Diario* concludes: "With this puerile proof the execution did not have to be delayed long and on the 17th of March they fell, in the same month that two years ago Bishop Oscar Arnulfo Romero was assassinated."

This tragedy has made Holland suffer with the poor and oppressed people of Central America. I hope and pray that this painful compassion will bring the people of El Salvador at least one step closer to peace.

Tuesday, March 23

This is my last day in Cuzco. John, Kathy, and I made a trip to the splendid Inca ruins in the area and to some churches and a museum in town. More than ever before, I was impressed by the majestic beauty of the buildings of the Inca Empire. The gigantic temples, the watchposts, and ritual baths were the work of a people guided by the rule, "Do not lie, do not steal, and do not be lazy," and inspired by a powerful devotion to the Sun God and many other divinities. But, more than before, I was stunned by the total insensitivity of the Spanish conquerors to the culture and religion they found here.

It suddenly hit me how radical Gustavo Gutiérrez's liberation theology really is, because it is a theology that starts with the people and wants to recognize the deep spirituality of the Indians who live in this land. How different from what we saw today on our trip. There we witnessed a centuries-long disregard for any Indian religiosity, and a violent destruction of all that could possibly be a reminder of the Inca Gods. What an incredible pretention, what a cruelty, what a sacrilegious sin committed by people who claimed to come in the name of a God of forgiveness, love, and peace.

I wished I had the time to spend a whole day just sitting on the ruins of Sacsahuamán. These temple ruins overlooking the city of

Cuzco, with its many churches built from its stones, make me ask the God of the sun, the moon, the stars, the rainbow, the lightening, the land, and the water to forgive what Christians did in his name.

Maybe the new spirituality of liberation is a creative form of repentance for the sins of our fathers. And I should not forget that these sins are closer to my own heart than I often want to confess. Some form of spiritual colonialism remains a constant temptation.

Wednesday, March 24
Lima, Peru

Today I flew back from Cuzco to Lima. I arrived just in time to commemorate the second anniversary of the martyrdom of Archbishop Oscar Romero of El Salvador. Since his death, tens of thousands of other Salvadorans have been murdered. They are the anonymous martyrs of our day. They are men and women who were killed because, in some way or another, they witnessed for freedom, human dignity, and a new society.

Often we think of martyrs as people who died in defense of their consciously professed faith, but Jesus' words, "What you did for the least of mine, you did for me," point to a true martyrdom in the service of God's people.

In a strange way, I am grateful that it is not only poor anonymous people who are losing their lives, but also well-known churchmen and churchwomen. The death of people like Bishop Romero allows us to lift up the martyrdoms of thousands of unknown *campesinos*, cathechists, youth leaders, teachers, priests, and guerrilla fighters, and to make them fruitful for the whole Christian community in Latin America. Bishop Romero's solidarity in death with the poor and oppressed of his country makes him a true bishop, not only in life, but also in death.

We celebrated Bishop Romero's death in the Church of Ciudad de Dios. I am increasingly impressed by the Christian possibility of celebrating not only moments of joy but also moments of pain, thus affirming God's real presence in the thick of our lives. A true Christian always affirms life, because God is the God of life, a life stronger than death and destruction. In him we find no reason to despair. There is always reason to hope, even when our eyes are filled with tears.

Many priests of the southern part of Lima joined Bishop Herman Schmidt in the celebration of the Eucharist. It was good to be back in these now-familiar surroundings. Many parishioners came up to me to express their joy at seeing me again after a few weeks of absence. I felt consoled by those whom I had known only for a short time. This mysterious experience in which grief and joy, gladness and sadness merged brought me to a new understanding of the unity of the death and resurrection of Christ.

Thursday, March 25

John Goldstein had asked me to take a letter to Troy Barette, the coordinator of the ministry of the Lutheran Church in America (LCA) in Peru. John and Kathy had already made me aware of how hard it is for Protestant missionaries to live and work in Peru. In the beginning of this century, Protestants were still outlawed, and the history of Protestantism shows periods of harsh persecution. Under the influence of a greater religious tolerance in the western world, and of a greater appreciation of the Protestant churches by the Second Vatican Council, outright persecution has stopped and some creative ecumenical dialogue has started. But from my own impressions, it seems that many Catholics have remained suspicious of Protestants, and some even overtly hostile toward them.

Such anti-Protestantism is partly understandable. Most priests have had disturbing experiences with different fundamentalist sects which are known for their fierce anti-Catholic preaching and for their divisive practices. Various evangelical sects—Jehovah's Witnesses, Mormons, Israelites, and similar groups—tend to create divisions between people, arouse an atmosphere of suspicion towards Catholics, and isolate people from their natural bonds with their relatives and friends. The great proliferation of these sometimes fanatic sects has certainly not built an ecumenical atmosphere between Catholics and Protestants.

But this being the case, there remains the fact that Protestantism has as much "right" to be in Peru as Catholicism and that there is, in fact, a relatively large, well-established Peruvian Protestant community. I am shocked by the argument that Catholicism is so much a part of the Peruvian culture that Protestantism, even in its most orthodox forms, can be seen only as robbing people of their own heritage. In the light of the way in which the Spanish destroyed the Indian cultures in Peru and imposed their religion on the people with the force of weapons—and this less than four hundred years ago—it seems quite preposterous to consider Protestantism a threat to the Peruvian culture. Moreover, the historic Catholic missionaries have never hesitated to evangelize alien cultures and to bring the Gospel to people for whom accepting the Good News of Jesus required a radical break with their traditions and customs. The history of the missions to China, Japan, and other well-integrated cultures shows clearly that cultural integrity has certainly not been the main concern of Catholic evangelizers in the past.

My discussions with John and Kathy, with Troy and Anne, and with many other Protestant missionaries from mainline denominations (Lutherans, Methodists, and Episcopalians) in Latin America have convinced me of the urgent need for a new ecumenism in the area of mission and for a much greater humility on the part of Catholics in their relationship with their Protestant brothers and sisters. It seems that there are now enough people on both sides who are open and ready for a creative collaboration.

Friday, March 26

This proved to be a very important day for me. As I had planned before going to Cuzco, I met again with Mattias Sienbenaller, the Luxembourgian priest who is pastor in Caja de Agua, one of Lima's *barrios*. This morning as we talked I felt that many pieces of my puzzle began to come together.

I explained to Mattias my dream about living among the people, praying with and for them, visiting them in their homes, offering days of retreat and recollection, and gradually helping them to articulate their own spiritual gifts. I asked him if he felt there was a place for me in Peru, how to relate all this to my past in Holland and the United States, and in which way to envision my future. I also shared with him my feelings about the clericalism in Peru, my need for a supportive community, and my search for ways to live a somewhat structured spiritual life with others.

Mattias responded with great warmth and concrete suggestions. He gave me a true sense of being called. He offered his own parish as a good place to try out what I was dreaming about. There is a good pastoral team that would offer support, encouragement, and constructive criticism; there is a daily life of communal prayer in the "rectory," a friendly home, and a strong spirit of working together. Moreover, the *barrio* Caja de Agua is close to the center of town and would make it easy to work closely with the people of Centro Bartolome de las Casas and to keep in touch with other pastoral events in town. Important for me was Mattias's insistence that I not cut off from all contact with the academic world in the United States. While he stressed that I should commit myself firmly to the Peruvian Church and be willing to work in the service of that Church, he also felt that it would be good to continue to communicate through writing and lecturing to the world from which I come. He therefore encouraged me to stay in touch with the places of theological formation in the States. Some part-time teaching there might be good for me, for the Church in Peru, and for students in the United States. Finally, we talked a little about introductions to the Cardinal of Lima, letters of recommendation, time schedules, and other such things.

It was quite a morning. Just three days before my return to the United States, an appealing, clear, and convincing vocation has started to take form. Many of the things Mattias proposed had a certain obviousness to me. The more I thought about them during the day, the more I felt that things fit very well and that I have as much clarity and certainty as I probably will ever have.

I now have to return to my friends in the States and to my bishop in Holland to ask for their responses and advice. Then I should soon be able to make a decision that has a solid basis and that is, I hope, not just an expression of my own will.

Saturday, March 27

My discussion with Mattias gave me a sense of closure. My stay in Peru is coming to an end, my impressions of ministry in Peru are starting to show patterns and my future plans are slowly taking some identifiable shape.

As I walked through Lima today, I had the strong sense that this city would become an important place for me in the future. I felt the desire to pray in this city at the different holy places and to ask God's guidance for my future. So I decided to go to the Church of the Lord of the Miracles. I still have vivid memories of my first Sunday in Peru, when I joined the crowd on the Plaza de Armas to welcome the procession of the Lord of the Miracles. This time I had a chance to see the painting on the main altar of the Church. Many people, young and old, men and women, were praying and I felt grateful that I could be there with them. As I looked up to the painting of the crucified Lord and felt the deep devotion of the people surrounding me, I had the feeling of being accepted in Peru. This, indeed, could become my country, my home, my church, and these people could become my fellow Christians, my friends, and my co-workers in the ministry. As my thoughts wandered to the future, I saw myself coming to this Church many times, asking the Lord of the Miracles to bless the people, to give me strength and courage, and to fill me with a spirit of joy and peace.

I also visited the house of St. Rose of Lima, observing where she lived her harsh and ascetic life, and the Church of La Merced, where the Cross of Pedro Urrarte is venerated. The streets and churches of Lima were all filled with people. I felt embraced by a welcoming city, and enjoyed just being carried along from place to place by the crowds. I did not feel like a stranger anymore. I felt more like a guest who was being invited to stay longer. My prayers became part of the murmuring sounds of the thousands who paraded through the streets and in and out of the churches. There was a sense of harmony, of belonging, yes, maybe even of vocation. To find that vocation, I had to come to Peru.

Sunday, March 28

Today during the Eucharist, we read in the letter to the Hebrews: "In the days when [Christ] was in the flesh, he offered prayers and supplications with loud cries and tears to God, who was able to save him from death, and he was heard because of his reverence. Son though he was, he learned obedience from what he suffered; and when perfected, he became the source of eternal salvation for all who obey him" (Heb. 5:7–9).

Jesus learned obedience from what he suffered. This means that the pains and struggles of which Jesus became part made him listen more perfectly to God. In and through his sufferings, he came to know God and could respond to his call. Maybe there are no better words than these to summarize the meaning of the option for the poor. Entering into the suffering of the poor is the way to become obedient, that is, a listener to God. Suffering accepted and shared in love breaks down our selfish defenses and sets us free to accept God's guidance.

After my stay in Bolivia and Peru I think that I have seen, heard, and even tasted the reality of this theology. For me it is no longer an abstract concept. My time with Sophia, Pablo, and their children was an experience that gave me a glimpse of true obedience. Living, working, and playing with them brought me close to a knowledge of God that I had not experienced anywhere before.

But do I really want to know the Lord? Do I really want to listen to him? Do I really want to take up my cross and follow him? Do I really want to dedicate myself to unconditional service?

I look forward to going home tomorrow, to sitting in a comfortable airplane. I like to be welcomed home by friends. I look forward to being back again in my cozy apartment, with my books, my paintings, and my plants. I like showers with hot water, faucets with water you can drink, washing machines that work, and lamps that keep burning. I like cleanliness. But is it there that I will find God? I look forward to being back at the Trappist monastery in upstate New York, to feeling the gentle silence of the contemplative life, singing the psalmodies in the choir, and celebrating the Eucharist with all the monks in the Abbey church. I look forward to walking again in the spacious fields of the Genesee Valley and driving through the woods of Letchworth Park. But is it there that I will find God? Or is he in this dusty, dry, cloud-covered city of Lima, in this confusing, unplanned, and often chaotic conglomeration of people, dogs, and houses? Is he perhaps where the hungry kids play, the old ladies beg, and the shoeshine boys pick your pocket?

I surely have to be where he is. I have to become obedient to him, listen to his voice, and follow him wherever he calls me. Even when I do not like it, even when it is not a way of cleanliness or comfort. Jesus said to Peter: "When you were young you put on your own belt and walked where you liked; but when you grow old you will stretch out your hands, and somebody else will put a belt round you and take you where you would rather not go" (John 21:18). Am I old enough now to be led by the poor, disorganized, unclean, hungry, and uneducated?

Monday, March 29

I am at the Lima airport. It is close to midnight. My flight is leaving at 1:00 A.M. At 6:30 A.M. I will be in Miami, at 10:15 A.M. in Washington, D.C., and at 2:05 P.M. in Rochester, New York. If all goes well, I will be at the Abbey around 3:30 P.M., just in time to celebrate the Eucharist with the monks. It is hard for me to comprehend this huge step from a restless airport in Peru to the restful monastery in upstate New York. My mind cannot yet do what the plane will do.

I feel grateful, deeply grateful. George-Ann Potter and her friend, Stephanie, came to the Maryknoll Center house to say good-bye. That meant a lot to me. We decided to have a little farewell party in a nearby restaurant. John and Cheryl Hassan, Larry Rich, Betty-Ann Donnelly, and Phil Polaski, Maryknoll lay missioners who happened to be at the Center house, joined in the celebration.

Just before we left the house, the city lights went out. We found our way to the restaurant in the pitch dark and sat around a large table with a candle in the middle. It felt like a mysterious conspiracy of friends.

This spontaneous last-minute get-together was a significant conclusion to my journey that started six months ago. It was as if these good friends were telling me, without planning to do so, that it would be possible to feel truly at home in Peru, to have good friends, to pray together, to share experiences and hopes, and to work in unity for the Kingdom of God. I felt a stronger bond with this small group of people huddled around the candle than I had felt with any other group during my stay in Peru. It felt as if these friends were answering the question that had occupied me during most of my stay here: Will there be a community in Peru that can give me a sense of belonging? Nobody in the casual, unpretentious, and unplanned gathering talked about community, at-homeness, or a sense of belonging, but to me all those present spoke a language that maybe only I could fully interpret. It was in that language that I heard a true invitation to return.

It is midnight now. The plane from Buenos Aires and Santiago has just arrived. I am eager to get on board and head north; but I am also aware that something has happened to me. I sit here and wonder if going north still means going home.

CONCLUSION
A Call to Be Grateful

The title of this journal summarizes what I found, learned, and heard. The word that I kept hearing, wherever I went, was: *Gracias!* It sounded like the refrain from a long ballad of events. *Gracias a usted, gracias a Dios, muchas gracias*—thank you, thanks be to God, many thanks! I saw thousands of poor and hungry children, I met many young men and women without money, a job, or a decent place to live. I spent long hours with sick, elderly people, and I witnessed more misery and pain than ever before in my life. But, in the midst of it all, that word lifted me again and again to a new realm of seeing and hearing: *"Gracias!* Thanks!"

In many of the families I visited nothing was certain, nothing predictable, nothing totally safe. Maybe there would be food tomorrow, maybe there would be work tomorrow, maybe there would be peace tomorrow. Maybe, maybe not. But whatever is given—money, food, work, a handshake, a smile, a good word, or an embrace—is a reason to rejoice and say *gracias.* What I claim as a right, my friends in Bolivia and Peru received as a gift; what is obvious to me was a joyful surprise to them; what I take for granted, they celebrate in thanksgiving; what for me goes by unnoticed became for them a new occasion to say thanks.

And slowly I learned. I learned what I must have forgotten somewhere in my busy, well-planned, and very "useful" life. I learned that everything that is, is freely given by the God of love. All is grace. Light and water, shelter and food, work and free time, children, parents and grandparents, birth and death—it is all given to us. Why? So that we can say *gracias,* thanks: thanks to God, thanks to each other, thanks to all and everyone.

More than anything else, I learned to say thanks. The familiar expression "let us say grace" now means something very different than saying a few prayers before a meal. It now means lifting up the whole of life into the presence of God and all his people in gratitude.

As I was trying to find an answer to the question: "Does God call me to live and work in Latin America?" I gradually realized that the word *"gracias"* that came from the lips of the people contained the answer. After many centuries of missionary work during which we, the people of the north, tried to give them, the people of the south, what we felt they needed, we have now come to realize that our very first vocation is to receive their gifts to us and say thanks. A treasure lies hidden in the soul of Latin America, a spiritual treasure to be recognized as a gift for us who live in the illusion of power and self-control. It is the treasure of gratitude that can help us to break through the walls of our individual and collective self-righteousness and can prevent us from destroying ourselves and our planet in the futile attempt to hold onto what we consider our own. If I have any vocation in Latin America, it is the vocation to receive from the people the gifts they have to offer us and to bring these gifts back up north for our own conversion and healing. The Maryknoll community in Peru speaks about "reverse mission," suggesting that the movement God wants us to learn is the movement from the south to the north. In the Latin America where countless martyrs have made the suffering Christ visible, a voice that we need to hear more than ever cries out. That voice calls us anew to know with heart and mind that all that is, is given to us as a gift of love, a gift that calls us to make our life into an unceasing act of gratitude.